You and Me

A Practical Guide for Meeting Your Teen with Faith, Hope, and Love

Nancy Washburn

Robert D. Reed Publishers . Bandon, OR

Robert D. Reed Publishers
P.O. Box 1992
Bandon, OR 97411
Phone: 541-347-9882; Fax: -9883
E-mail: 4bobreed@msn.com
Website: www.rdrpublishers.com

Editor: Cleone Reed
Book Cover Designer: Eric and Nicol Nishioka
Book Designer: Amy Cole

Paperback ISBN: 978-1-944297-40-4
eBook ISBN: 978-1-944297-41-1

Library of Congress Number: 2018914762

Designed and Formatted in the United States of America

DEDICATION

To my children, Andy, Spencer, and Natalie,
who have taught me about life and love.

To my parents who gave me faith, hope, and love.

ACKNOWLEDGMENTS

How does a book come to be? It starts in the heart, moves to the head, and then to the fingers. I want to thank the people who stirred my heart and those who moved it from my head to my hands.

In my case it would have never moved without my partner in crime and love, Hayward Nishioka, a writer himself, and a judo champion and icon. Many days we spent writing together: he in his world, me in the world of parenting teenagers.

He humbly takes no credit but deserves all the recognition for making me sit still, reading each day's work, and encouraging me that these were messages that parents needed to hear. My heart knows this work would have lingered only in my classroom and heart without him. I thank him so much for his quiet but steady push!

There is no greater honor than sharing life with others, and it has been my privilege to walk that path with literally thousands of students and parents. Each person added to my life and understanding, sometimes breaking my heart with their stories, sometimes making me stand in awe of the power people have inside to right their life in the face of adversity. I appreciate their openness and trust.

I want to thank another writer friend and amazing woman, Jo Quici, for being the first person willing to take her time to look at my beginning forays and editing some feeble attempts. Thanks, Jo!

Thank you to my daughter Natalie for being the first to read the entire book and helping me to format, formulate ideas, and of course for letting me share her life so publicly! She is so competent; I always take her thoughts quite seriously. To be around her is like a serene walk in the forest, refreshing and calming.

Linda Flynn, also a first reader, brought her expert support and encouragement along with her lovely friendship and I want to thank her for it all.

Eric and Nicol Nishioka deserve my heartfelt thanks for using their talents and professions of art and design to hang in there with me to create a cover that fits my imagination and that I love! They are a loving couple besides and excellent parents to Naya, both qualities that I admire.

Amy Cole is another wonder who has added so much to my words by making them look beautiful and sensible. Thank you, Amy!

Lastly, I want to thank Bob and Cleone Reed and their publishing company for taking an interest in my messages and believing that books and ideas can change the world. I feel enveloped by their support and expertise. Thank you so much!

TABLE OF CONTENTS

The Three Messages

THE ROAD AHEAD—AGENDA

Often in my college classes I begin by telling my students briefly what we will be doing in the class that day—a verbal agenda. Some people feel more secure when they can see a little bit down the road of time. The preparation helps us all to be on the same page or planet!

What is my agenda, here, in this book?

Simply to change your mind, so that you will have empathy for what adolescents are feeling and living through these years, and you will know what they need from you.

For a number of years, I have been teaching these ideas in my Community College classes. Each semester I have many eighteen- and nineteen-year-olds, and sometimes even actual high school students. Our campus is extremely diverse and always many, many students say, "I wish my parents knew this." Often, I will notice students tearing up when I talk about the teenage years and what they need. I want to pass it on!

Through the years, as I have worked in the field of parenting or teaching, basically preparing folks to work with children and adolescents effectively, and through hearing so many stories and through raising my own three children, my heart began to ache for adolescents. I believe our culture perpetuates and supports a misunderstanding of these years and that essentially, they get a bad rap.

Unfortunately, we are all about thirteen inside. We can become just as insecure or obnoxious if challenged and sink to a rebellious stance and push our child away. With awareness, and some particular skills, we can learn to love them in a way that *shows*, that is accessible to them.

BEING YOU

Oprah Winfrey has made a career (and fortune) based on the idea that you should value who you are. Many spiritual teachers propose that finding the *true* self may be one of the goals of life, possibly the primary goal.

I'm happy with the fact that my three grown children have all chosen very diverse careers, and none of them what their father or I chose. I like the idea that, evidently, we allowed them the space to be who they wanted to be, at least partially.

Clearly, we are as unique as snowflakes or leaves—clearly even identical twins put a different spin on their lives—not to discount all the similarities that being a person entails, or a snowflake, or leaf.

So, it is a small leap to claim that we all have a potential that we can fulfill. When children are born and given what they need, they are more likely to be people who are adding to society in some way. When children are harmed emotionally, they may become someone who takes from others, hurts others, or harms society. They will be anti-social, against social functioning. You and I want our neighbors, colleagues, in-laws, auto mechanics, etc. to be people we can trust to add to social relations, dependable and helpful. But there is more.

My mom always used to say that when she saw a person living on the street, she always thought, "This person was once someone's baby." I know whoever you are, no person thinks, "I hope I raise someone who will be homeless or I hope I raise someone who will hurt other people." What happens?

What about your children's teacher or your future doctor? I imagine you hope they are ethical and kind and really love what they do. I believe you probably want them to be suited for the job and even have a *calling* to do it.

Someone may raise a child someday who will discover a cure for aids or cancers we haven't defeated. Who will that be? I believe it will be a person that was able to reach their full potential, someone who was allowed to flower, who got most of what they needed as a child in the emotional realm. It won't mean they had a perfect childhood or didn't have challenges. Remember, people can get through anything IF they have the social-emotional support they need. The challenges themselves are positive. But it won't be someone who was harmed by life so completely that they hurt others or harm society either. We need to know enough as the adults on the planet to show children how to be a person and then step back and let them tell us who they are.

Never before on the planet, never again,
there's no one like you.

EVERY TEENAGER NEEDS...
THREE MESSAGES

When I was a young teenager, there was a hit song by the Beach Boys called "In my Room." It was a song about finding solace and finding a place to *tell my troubles to.* This need for a place of safety is a human need, of course, but during the particular upheaval of adolescence it is not easily come by. As adults we know we are in charge of our own lives: we know we have power, we've made some things happen before, we have perspective, we know sometimes you win and sometimes you lose, and it's the way of the world. It reminds me of the old adage, "'Wherever you go there you *are.'* A teen has very few places that truly feel safe, and inside themselves is often not one of them. The people around them are somewhat suspect too. How can we help them to come to the realization that it is safe inside oneself, that the human doubts and questions are just that, human, not unique to them but part of the common human condition?

Furthermore, the questions can't kill you.

THE THREE MESSAGES

As parents you want to give your child the best of life; in order to give them the best you need to provide, *three emotional underpinnings* for them:

Love

1. But more than love, *I like you. I'm crazy about you. I pursue you, I cherish you.*

   You are a person I like to be around.

Faith

2. *I accept you, your choices, styles, friends, and need for independence. I trust you.*

   Your choices have meaning.

Hope

3. *I won't give up on you, your problems, ups and downs, choices and even mistakes. For "what I see in you…" I will hold the hope for you through this turbulent time.*

   You are right where you are supposed to be.

IF, THEN...

In your home lives an adolescent. "What happened to my sweet little girl?" one friend asked lately as her child became a twelve-year-old. A teacher friend with many years of experience who works with sixth graders told me that after Valentine's Day they magically begin to be the teenagers we have come to know.

We're not making something up when we witness dramatic changes taking place between childhood and adolescence. But what to do: throw up your hands, turn into an adolescent yourself, hunker down and wait until it passes, become very controlling of their activities?

I propose that to remain and/or become an effective support to our young person, there are three messages that we need to foster, vital ways of being with our teenager to flag them through the course with excellent results as they finally move toward the open field of adulthood.

These messages may sound simple at first, but I think you will agree as you delve in that the complexity of *acting them out* is as challenging as love. Feelings are easy; even thoughts can be easy, but acting in ways that communicate love, support, and understanding can get as muddled as a Twister game. Many examples and stories to follow illustrate how, when, and why to give your young person the gift of these messages in practical contexts.

The emotional messages teenagers need to receive from those around them are:

1. I like you, I cherish you. I pursue you, even as you turn toward the world. You are a person I like to be around. **Love**

2. I accept you. I accept your choices. Your choices have meaning. I have faith in you. **Faith**

3. I won't give up on you. You are right where you are supposed to be. **Hope**

These are not merely spoken messages of course, but actions; and the skills to live them are to follow. Be ready to jump; the ski lift is moving, and they are way ahead of you!

The story I want to tell is about adolescents—yours, mine, and ours. The story is painful and funny and oh, so very important. The struggles are real, the challenges many, the rewards for effort a far-off goal. There is no instant gratification in parenting a teen, but the value we place on our children knows no bounds. Early on in our development as a species, herbal remedies developed and were passed on for healing. Stories, too, have filtered through time to teach lessons that were not for entertainment, like a good read but for survival. The aloe developed correctly can stop the itch; the stories can aid the healing. So, pull up your chair to the fire while we reveal the types of faith, hope, and love needed for your child's and your survival and how to effectively provide them.

Returning home from my first foray of driving lessons with my oldest child behind the wheel, I went to my bedroom and lay in the fetal position and had this thought. *Possibly older people get gray hair not from simply aging, but from putting a fifteen-year-old behind the wheel of a heavy vehicle that can maim and kill.* Even responsible teens cause our heart to pound and our muscles to tense. Even in this common scenario, the parent has a challenge not to let their child hurt themselves or anyone else and yet be encouraging, instructive, and supportive, all the while being fearful oneself. No small test and yet not even one of the main challenges of parenting a teen. Just because of the fact of all the developmental milestones, the parenting-teenagers road is rocky whether you are driving a luxury car or a beat-up clunker. If you know how to drive, you can pretty much step into any vehicle and figure it out. So, our focus in this book is *how to*, principles, that can override other factors to guarantee the *three emotional messages* are delivered.

You will learn how to build a relationship of trust and faith, hope, and love for your teenager, a person you would jump in front of a truck to save but who can also make you crazy with worry and fear. You will learn practical skills and ways to talk to and monitor your child to build what they need considering their physical, mental, and emotional stages of development.

It's always been my belief that humans can get through anything and come out emotionally healthy if, and it's a big IF, they have the needed support. Once getting my nails done, a Vietnamese woman of my own age told me, as we both cried, of how she had seen her mother, father, and brother killed in front of her when she was eight years old during the Vietnam War. A doctor friend lost his whole family in the killing fields of Cambodia. They lived and became productive citizens with loving families of their own.

There is a song with the popular lyrics that state whatever doesn't kill you makes you stronger. This CAN be true, but we all know stories of people who have not become stronger through hardship but have given up into alcohol, drugs, or suicide.

The difference is human support of a kind that is other oriented. Allowing the person to process what happened in a loving and accepting environment, and as long as needed, provides the soil for integrating experiences into our personal worldview. Understanding what is happening physically, emotionally, and mentally in adolescents will give us the foundation to know how to do the IF. The developmentally vulnerable time of the adolescent has particular types of support needs which we will be dissecting here.

Many people believe that love is enough to raise a healthy child, but after working with hundreds of families over several decades I am here to tell you love is not enough. Our goal as parents and as a society is to raise children who reach their full potential and add to society and do not take away from society. Undoubtedly, this process takes skills. These stories are meant to be illustrative of these processes, a practical guide to providing what teenagers need to be healthy now and to grow into healthy adults. Take a deep breath; help is on the way!

What Is Happening To Me? Typical Teen Development

IN THE BEGINNING, THERE WAS PUBERTY

When people discover you are a parent and then ask how old your child is, if you state any time in the teenage years, especially the younger teens, the person generally takes on an empathetic demeanor. "Oh, poor you", or a "That's a hard age" usually follows. When people pass the high school or junior high they usually are critical of what they see, "Why do they dress like that, listen to that music, have tattoos, long hair, baggy pants, nose rings... etc." You name the time in the past fifty years and it's always the same, different specifics, same theme; teenagers are a world unto themselves and it's a weird world. Teenagers are given a wide berth of derogatory looks and comments. The adults raising them or teaching them have similar views in many ways. The average adolescent hears eighty percent negative comments when they step outside of their home, from peers, teachers and the general society. If an adult heard eighty percent negative at work they would have been fired, slit their wrists, or at the very least be looking for a new job. Teenagers get a bad rap in society and that's a fact.

NEGATIVE IN NEGATIVE OUT

At what most psychologists would agree is the most difficult developmental time of life, many young people are getting the least support in any part of their lives. What impact can this have on a young person?

What is developmentally going on for them? What messages can we give to adolescents to make the trip to adulthood a more productive and positive time and provide a more positive outcome for the young person? In order to understand the depth of this period of life, a little developmental delving is necessary.

Developmental Psychologists have been observing children for many generations to determine what happens as we grow, and what is typical? Looking at what we know so far about how young people typically develop in the physical, social-emotional, and the cognitive areas is an important foundation for how we interact and support teenagers. We will begin with the physical hurricane that is blowing through the bodies of young teens.

PUBERTY SNEAKS IN LIKE A LION

Growth hormones are surging through their bodies. It feels as if their bodies betray themselves by its constant changing against their will. I've known boys to grow three inches in one summer! Breasts appear, and men are looking at girls in new uncomfortable or powerful ways that they have no experience to handle. Young men can't depend on their own voice. I remember people calling my home, and they would think my thirteen-year-old son was ME on the phone. Boys are supposed to become men and people think they have an adult woman's voice!? The world tells teens, "You are a woman now or you are a man now" and yet they feel like a kid with a new body that just feels uncomfortable. Think of Alice in Wonderland!

Once in line for a movie I stood behind three teenage girls about 15 years old. They all looked young and lovely, but one of them was exceptionally pretty. Their conversation went like this:

> Girl #1: Are you going to Melanie's birthday party?
> Girl #2: Yeah".
> Girl #3: (the pretty one) "I wasn't invited."
> Girls #1 and #2: "Why not?"
> Girl #3: "Melanie told me I was too pretty."

Well, we all know what that means. Melanie didn't want any competition with the boys and they talked about that a bit. What was running through my mind was: *How is one supposed to become a woman with these messages being given? After all, you are supposed to be pretty, but evidently not too pretty or you won't have girlfriends. Sounds like you lose either way. Is this what it means to be a woman? How does a fifteen-year-old integrate this into her new changing body and her perception of roles?* Confusing isn't it?

Many parents might say something like, "It doesn't matter what other people think." But it does when you are fifteen. What would be more helpful?

Women understand at a fundamental level the hormone thing. Any woman knows that hormone changes can make you feel totally depressed even when you know intellectually your life is fine. The power of feelings being controlled by hormones is something you can understand over time, but when it is new as a teenager, there is no knowledge or experience to cope. A hormone surge at another moment can make you feel elated with flushed cheeks and dancing around the house higher than a kite, all from the powerful chemicals we know as hormones. I have heard it said that behavior that would be considered mental illness at any other age is considered normal for teens.

Much of this perception by others comes from hormones and the physical changes of this period. It is a transitional time. Transitions in and of themselves are challenging, but when the body changes catapult you into a new world, out-of-control disruption is inevitable. Seemingly out of nowhere, you feel awkward around the boys you played kickball with last summer. A new self-consciousness emerges driven much by body changes and body-image adjustments. If you watch even young toddlers, children test their bodies learning what spaces they can fit into and how far they can reach onto a table to knock things down. Testing the body as a teenager is the *normal* thing to do with all these new feelings and new perceptions. If I am getting catcalls as I walk down the street, I might hide my body, or I might dress provocatively just to see what this body can elicit in the world.

If anyone has ever been judged by physical appearance alone, you know it takes years to come to terms with such outside perceptions of your inside reality. Some sources have said that self-esteem at any age is most related to body image. What then for teens when the body image is going through tsunami-type changes? So even if we were only considering physical changes, we should feel great empathy and understanding for teens. But there is so much more! The whole cognitive/intellectual aspect of a teen is also in the throes of an earthquake!

WHY AM I HERE? HOW ADOLESCENTS THINK!

I remember lying in bed at night and semi-freaking out thinking about *living forever,* after one dies. In the Catholic tradition in which I was raised, the belief was that you have *eternal life.* Greater scholars than I have written at some length about the meaning of those words, but all I knew as a young person was that it was creepy and hard to imagine. Although unaware of the process going on within me then, now I realize that I was being catapulted into what Jean Piaget, an influential Swiss psychologist, calls formal operational thought. In this last stage of Piaget's theory of four stages of cognitive development, Piaget posits that our development can be tracked by HOW we think.

The physical body is out of control and the mind is to follow. For the first time in a child's life, he/she is thinking about the big questions: *Why am I here? Is there a God? What is the purpose of life?* Many of these questions are the human questions that every person eventually grapples with. The problem for teenagers is that this is the FIRST time they are capable of thinking about these questions. Consequently, with no theory or practice, the questions come into the adolescent consciousness and cause anxiety. In life THIS is where real loss of innocence takes place. When you reach formal operational thought, you are no longer a child; you are as capable of intricate, abstract, hypothetical thought as your dad or grandmother or teacher. Then why do we look down on teenagers? Their thought is just as complex as ours. The issue is what they lack, and that is experience. Any adult can tell you, experience is a great teacher.

Formal operational thought has another characteristic. When you enter this stage, you realize that your parents are not the only holders of the truth. Before this cognitive stage, you pretty much think your parents know everything. I remember becoming aware that my parents didn't know everything. I had two feelings simultaneously: a smug realization that I had been right and a query that goes like this: *If they don't know, who does?*

We get to the planet and we begin our theory building. It is written in every fiber, that our quest is to find out all we can about the planet we have been placed on and how it works. As children, even as very young ones, we begin to develop theories about the world, people, processes, things. We attempt to make connections and begin to see our place and purpose on the planet as we go along. Theories develop about the world outside of us and the world within our own mind.

Teenagers' particular developmental stage pushes them to form an identity of who they are. The experiences up to this point are foundational, but now they are capable of fully understanding the world within and prescribing its parameters in terms of one individual life, apart from all the others who have had input up until this point.

Just as the new body and physical feelings can initiate conversation and empathy, the new thought processes should do the same. These changes are real and faced by everyone. We don't have to wonder if they are feeling these things; we don't have to wait for them to tell us what they are feeling. We as supportive sensei (a person who goes before), have to address these issues with our teens. More to follow on how, but for now realize these changes are monumental for a young person.

This ability is new and overwhelming at times, and from a teen's view, comes out of nowhere. One quick way to equalize the playing field is to explain this process of development to them. Feeling *normal* helps them to keep things in perspective.

POSSIBILITIES—FORMAL OPERATIONAL THOUGHT

The rude awakening, the endless possibility, the limits, the knowledge that life doesn't always work out the way people have dreamed about.... these are the realizations of formal operational thought, the stage of cognitive development described by Jean Piaget in which teenagers find themselves in the developmental process.

An awareness arises that different people do things differently. There are possibilities beyond the experiences I have had thus far as a teenager—possibilities in thinking, in action, in philosophy, in beliefs.

I overheard a nine-year-old speaking about his father one day and he said, "My dad is so strong; he could win any fight." At fifteen you know your dad has limits. He may be strong, you may still admire him, but now you are aware your father is probably not the strongest man in the world.

In my teenage years Henry Kissinger was sent to negotiate a peace between Palestine and Israel. I believed he must be a very intelligent man. But the peace did not last as we know today. I remember thinking in a fearful way, *if the best minds we have can't figure this out, then who can?* It was frightening to become aware in a very real way of human limits on a broad scale. These are formal operational processes, realizations that lead to a loss of an innocence of a sort; realizations though, that also lead to many more options than a younger child can fathom.

How does a young person decide to believe that being honest is a value they want to be a part of their identity? They now know and probably have experienced dishonesty and consequences of this that may look positive and consequences that may look negative. How do they decide about their personal approach to drugs? They know people who take drugs with negative effects, but they probably also know some people who use drugs with seemingly no negative effects. How do they make a decision to be sexually active? Some young people have sex with no pregnancy, disease, emotional trauma; others do not.

How do we help them in the new world of formal operational thought to maneuver through all this input or this new processing system?

Innovation comes from possibility, so possibility is usually a very positive concept. Think of formal operational thought as a new skill. The knowledge that there are many ways to build your own life, your own theories, your own identity, is qualitatively new thinking. Hypothetical thought is new to you at this stage.

For instance, the following is an example of what an adolescent might be thinking and learning as they build a theory on drugs or alcohol:

a. Watched people act out of control at a party and didn't want to be in that position myself.

b. Some people who did it seemed sad or lost; they didn't seem happy about themselves.

c. Some people who did drugs didn't seem like they had that much going for them.

d. I knew you could get addicted, and the feeling of that controlling me seemed scary.

e. People died by jumping off a building or doing some dangerous thing while high.

f. Some people seemed to lose motivation in their lives. Later I saw the addicts as not *there* for their family or people who loved them.

g. Gene died of an overdose.

The budding theory was based on the information I had and of course been told, and very much by my own experience and what I wanted my life to be like, and also by fear. At this age we are building theories that we will take forward into adult life because we are now thinking like an adult because of our development and physiology.

The best theories are built on knowing lots of possibilities. How do I know if I like sushi unless I've tried it? If I don't like fish or rice or seaweed, then I have some information about whether I will like sushi. If the idea of eating raw fish is foreign to me and seems the opposite of my experience with fish, psychologically I might be predisposed not to like it. And still, I might actually like it when I try it. My theory can get input from small pieces of information, from experience, culture, expectations, and what I have heard and seen from others' experiences.

DO GOOD, FEEL GOOD

As a teenager at my Catholic school, one of the requirements was to do a certain number of hours of volunteer work. One of my choices was to work at a convalescent home talking with elderly people. I also worked as a candy striper at a local hospital. Each of these experiences helped me to form my identity. Through experience I was able to look at my preferences and get feedback about my personality and talents. As these experiences and many others blended together, I was able to know that I am a people person. This fact is part of my identity, part of who I say that I am. My approach to the world then reflects this belief about who I am.

Along with talking to teenagers about experiences and having them explore ideas with others, we need to give them opportunities to act in the world. They are primed to do this anyway, but *where* do we want them to act in the world? By focusing their activity, we can expose them to situations that help them to learn who they are and what they believe. Do we want our teens just out on the streets of the neighborhood with other teens or do we want them involved in productive activities?

The Search Institute has developed Forty Developmental Assets that young people need to be successful and resilient. They surveyed research to glean these resiliency factors. One of them is that the young person feels safe at home, school, and in the neighborhood. Another is that the young person serves in the community at least one hour a week. These assets are what help teens to have the resiliency to withstand the negative experiences that life inevitably hands them. www.search-institute.org.

As parents and teachers and even as schools we can provide opportunities for activities and require young people to be involved in something outside of schoolwork. The list can be quite varied: sports, dance, choir, plays, yearbook, band, student government at the school. But if your child does not fit in or join these activities, the family can require volunteering, work in a youth group at a church, or an actual job in the community. The message must be that you have to do something with your time.

These involvements have several other positive effects on the child. Usually there are other adult mentor opportunities, like coaches or bosses in these situations, and the child has a chance to discover their talents. They receive the satisfaction of helping others or earning a paycheck or producing a product that others appreciate. It gives them a chance to build skills and relationships of productivity and working together for a common goal, all skills needed in family life and the work world. A *do good, feel good* follows. Our *actions* are what build our feelings of ourselves.

A middle-aged colleague of mine, who had no children of his own, once came back from visiting his nephew at a prestigious college. He commented that now he knew the largest untapped natural resource in the United States. With a straight face he said, "College students." In his visit he noted that these highly intelligent, skilled young people were spending a lot of time playing video games and just *hanging out.* Amusing as it may be, we have to wonder about the truth of this statement.

Our stance has to not be, "Do you want to do something?" Instead, it needs to be, "On what do you want to spend your time?" As with the two-year-old being potty trained, we learned not to say as he dances around, "Do you need to go potty?" Instead, we say, "Here we go to the potty."

I learned this lesson with my own children when I wanted them to help clean the house. When I said, "OK, you clean the bathroom and you sweep the kitchen floor etc.," they would complain. When I made a list of the chores and said, "Which one would you like to do?" they chose one. Expectations are a powerful thing!

So *what* they want to do is their choice, but no chore is not a choice.

"GOOD KIDS"

Recently in a coffee shop I bumped into a woman I know casually. Asking about her family led to the fact that her children were now teenagers. The empathetic look on my face led her to offer that her son was doing very well at a local Catholic high school and that he is a *good kid* and there were no problems. Often, I have found, when parents say that, they mean that their child is not a caricature of teenage difficulties, rebelliousness, drugs, alcohol, no communication, or sexual issues in which the parents feel the need to intervene.

As we talked, and she became more comfortable, she began to tell me that he was very upset though about his baseball team. He was a good player but was being put down by other team members because he is small and younger. This may sound like an everyday growing-up story and it is, but he was thinking of dropping the team, based on his teammate's comments alone. She had several talks with him and listened well.

He's a *good kid* and the pitfall of a good kid can be that we are *hands off.*

No matter the person, the quest of the teenage time is to find this identity that is something they hold to and can claim as their own. At this point we gather up all the little pieces of our life so far—the genetics and the myriad experiences—and we form them into "a me" that will venture forward into adulthood. As a teenager, though, you don't necessarily know this is your day job. You only feel these forces within and without pulling you and playing with your feelings like a tease. No matter how conventional the child's behavior on the outside, there is a whirlwind within. Like a diver assessing the clarity of the water by the color on top, like a hang glider judging the direction of the wind from the top of the mountain, like predicting the flow of traffic in LA without your GPS, you can be so wrong if you only observe one aspect of the situation.

Through our training we have been taught to be polite and to not bother people with our internal feelings. We protect ourselves, and rightly so, from criticism by keeping much of ourselves only to be shared with a few people we trust. For example, when I met a man I knew on the street weeks before he committed suicide, with me, he acted as if everything in his life was fine.

The *good kid* is having struggles too, especially the teenage kid, without the ability necessarily to seek the support they need. When you are trying to become an adult, sometimes you have the false sense that adulthood means handling everything on your own. My two-year-old grandson told me this morning, "Grandma, you know everything." I set him straight of course, but children believe adults do. Adolescents begin to know the truth, but remember, it's a process and therefore they are in flux. I know now that the only people who look like they have it all together are people you don't know well enough yet! The new evolutionary studies and sensibilities, as a matter of fact, seem to point to the fact that what aided survival was cooperation, not just an independent *fittest* person or animal, as has been some of the focus in the past.

All kids need effective parenting; the skills are learned and applied deliberately until they become second nature. It is about putting what you know and feel in your head and heart into a format that a teenager or child can understand and hear. As you will discover later, this child may need to be introduced to the decision-making process. He needs his feelings validated, saying, for example, "That's a big decision you have to make there, to quit or not, since I know you love baseball so much." He is getting the listening, but he might need a story of how you made a decision in the past. He DOES NOT need *your* answer. The moment to teach process, is here, but subtlety with no *teachy-preachy* overtones, but as an exploration. Reflect back what he is saying, "You think you will quit baseball because of the teasing." Ask if he has thought of other options perhaps, but after you have proven to him that it is *his decision*. Maybe you can say how you feel later, much later, but not in a way that makes you seem invested in the outcome, but perhaps, "I don't like to see you give up something you like so much."

HELP, I NEED SOMEBODY!

Yesterday I was representing the Child and Family Studies Department at a career day at a local inner-city high school. Students came up to my table in all their myriad fashions reflective of their personality. Some came with very interested expressions, asking relevant questions. Others shied away and stood back until I engaged them. Still others came up and started playing with the magnet toys I had brought to draw them in. Most came in groups of two or three, but I noticed the most interested ones didn't necessarily travel in a pack. Each of us is clearly unique, formed by genetics and, also, everything that has happened to us since sperm invaded egg, including the way in which we interact with the world.

But what struck me more was how similar teenagers can be to each other. Even though we are individuals, life has stages. Erik Erikson* describes psychosocial stages that cover the life span, in other words, ways that we interact in the social and internal world to figure out how to resolve a conflict for that stage so that we can move on to the next phase with psychological health. The teenagers, your grandmother, and I all have our own spin on life; but the questions we are looking to answer are also driven by stages reflected somewhat by age or where we have been so far. Anyone who has spent any time with a two-year-old knows that they want to do things on their own. Anyone who has been with a young teenager realizes they want to fit in with their peers.

The teenagers looked to each other as they asked and answered questions, to see how they were being received by their peers. Most didn't know what they wanted to do with their life as far as work, and all were very concerned about the other young people around them. Finding a mate, finding a calling or something to do with one's life are all part of this stage of growth, *Who Am I?* It is not like any other time in the life cycle. Neither your grandma nor your ten-year-old are asking this question. When there are so many fundamental internal questions all at once, we are disrupted. Anywhere at any high school I would have seen similar behavior. It's developmental, in other words a combination of actual physical brain development and the biological and social processes brought to bear on the adolescent that illicit certain similar types of behavior. They are not adults, but they are on the cliff of adulthood.

What are we doing at the bottom to support a safe landing into the next phase?

In judo practice the first thing they teach is how to fall. This may inform our practice to give young people strategies for life.

When my middle son was sixteen, he came to me and said, "How do I get a job?" Honestly my first thought looking at this 6' foot 4" child of mine was, *you don't know how to look for a job?* My next thought was, *why would he? He has never done it before.* Then I thought, *looks like a man, not a man.* None of this did I say to my son, of course.

I listed strategies for getting a job. You dress nicely, look them in the eye, shake their hand, and look like you REALLY want a job. As a teenager you may not have a lot to offer yet in the realm of experience, so you need to look honest, sincere, and hard working. I have been places when some teens walk in looking for jobs with a friend dressed in their baggy jeans and just say, "Do you have a job?" No one is at the top of the cliff with them or on the mat teaching them how to fall, or how to soar.

Strategies for life skills are a way we can give the gift that keeps on giving. Strategies you can apply to a similar situation later or to a new situation. Whenever anyone says to me, "It's easy," I always think, *yes, it's easy if you know how. If you don't know how, then it might not be easy.* Strategies are ways to make life easier, ways we help people *know how* in a way that guides them but doesn't do it for them.

Just this past weekend in the airport, I was trying to make the water run in an automatic faucet. I always thought there was a little sensor in the back somewhere, so I always just wave my hands around and up and down. I am often not very successful, and it takes a while, or I change faucets. There I am waving away. I ask the young woman next to me and she puts her hand under and gets water. Then I try it and nothing. She then says, "You have to put your hand up closer to the spout." Bingo! Strategy! It works every time. Now I KNOW and it's easy! It was difficult for me before because I didn't know the strategy, yes, an easy strategy, but if you don't know it, it doesn't matter how easy it is!

*Erik Erikson was a developmental Psychologist and Psychoanalyst, a student of Sigmund Freud who expanded our understanding of the social influences on development beyond merely psychosexual aspects. In developing an eight-stage theory of psychosocial development that spans our entire life, Erikson describes a controversy that needs to be resolved at each stage to continue to grow in a healthy manner.

I WANNA BE ME — THE DRESS

In my little world as a teenager, my mom would go with me to buy clothes. I was tall and chubby so shopping with my friends was not that fun for me because they were all cute and small. I also did not have a sister to shop with and my mom was not particularly into clothes. But later in my teenage years I lost some weight and was feeling much better about myself. I went clothes shopping by myself for the first time that I remember. Clothes shopping was not something that made me feel good about myself in the past. But this time I found a long dress, maroon with stitching on the bodice, and I felt so pretty in it. I was so excited about feeling attractive and about choosing something wonderful on my own and paying for it with my own money.

I brought the dress home and showed my mom, so eager to share my joy. I could tell the minute she looked at it that she did not like it. She made a slightly negative comment I recall. I think she said, "Where do you think you can wear that?" I was deflated inside. I don't think I ever said anything to her, but I remember the feeling so well all these years later. It was as if my pride in myself and my choices had been denigrated. I even questioned in my mind the purchase of the dress, even though I loved it so much. Could she be right? I wanted her to be pleased for me. I needed her validation as a woman, a model. One small rite of passage that I was experiencing had been stepped on. My mom is gone now so I can't check with her to see how, or if, she remembers that day, but I know it was not as meaningful to her as to me.

The opportunity was missed to support my growing sense of my own identity by the experience of making choices and being able to receive positive feedback for my choices. At best she could have said, "You have your own sense of style." At the least she could have reflected back to me how I felt. "You feel excited about choosing this dress."

We don't have to agree with our young person's choices. We don't have to have our way, especially in choices that don't impact their future lives in some dramatic way. We need to acknowledge the growing sense they have of themselves. Through choices our teenagers are expressing themselves in the world. One fundamental way one expresses identity is through choices, *I'm this and not that. I like this and not that.* Especially in the neutral areas we need to support their choices and the ability and courage it takes to make a choice. Of course, they know we are watching. It is the process that needs support and validation, the choice process, the initiative process.

It is odd about parents, but we don't want our children to necessarily *go along with the crowd* or be unduly influenced by other teenagers, but we want them to cave into our choices with no questions asked. The whole point of identity formation is to ask the questions and decide who one will be, separate from the parent.

Once I listened to Robert Fulghum talk about having teenagers. He expressed the idea that sometimes we hold back some of our thoughts from our children, of course, just as we do with anyone we love. For example, when your pimply teenager feels badly about their skin, you hopefully wouldn't even think of saying anything negative to them about it. In regard to other choices, many parents let out judgmental words or even facial expressions. I am suggesting that we support the process of making choices. It's the attempt and the outcome where the learning takes place, that which we call experience, which leads to better choices generally, or at least more studied choices.

A helpful response to emerging identity would be to ask the child to elaborate on their choice or to just accept it without any negative vibe. Think of your favorite flower or beverage and you can see that we are unique and have preferences that may be inborn. No one made you have a favorite flower; you just like some better than others. Our choices on many things are just more of this, expressing who we are. Many of our choices are learned, of course, by a life of reinforcement, modeling, and other influences; but they are reflective of us.

My father often said this Latin phrase, "De gustibus est disputandum." The meaning is, "Concerning taste there shall be no dispute."

It is not just preference we are talking about with teenagers, though; it is the confidence to form identity and the support to do so from those around you. The cheering crowd around the toddler using the potty for the first time can be the same cheering crowd around the choices that teenagers make. If we have talked with them openly and honestly to this point, their important choices will be more aligned with our values anyway; and the less important choices, in terms of content, will be ways of validating the emerging adult.

I kept that dress for many, many years and wore it until it fell apart, but I always remembered the feelings I had had in sharing my jubilant moment with my mom. A chance was missed to support emerging identity by a loving parent.

A WHOLE NEW ME

Along with the questions of *What happened to my body* and *Why are my thought processes so distressing and complicated*, within a few short years I am to answer in all its complexity the question, *Who Am I?*

Internally, psychologically, socially trudging into the teenage years, Eric Erikson tells us that the adolescent must resolve the conflict of identity vs. role confusion. What is *normal* for the teenager is to be struggling with his own identity. Unless he comes to terms with a sense of himself as separate from others with particular ideas, beliefs, values, morals—in other words, theories—he will be confused about who he is and unable to move forward to become a productive person in the world.

Identity is a view of oneself that is internally consistent. That's a tall order for any of us. I need to decide what I believe about sex, drugs, rock and roll, and begin to act upon those beliefs in the world. This daunting task has been forgotten by most adults. They believe that the young person needs to listen to them and they will be able to save them a lot of trouble. Young people's job at this age is to develop theories. A theory is a framework for understanding. Within a few short years, they need to develop theories about roles, what it means to be a man or a woman, vocation, drugs, alcohol, music, religion, etc.

The scariest thing about teenagers for adults is the result of this theory building. How does an intelligent person develop a theory? By experimentation, of course! Therein lies the fear. Experimenting as a teenager can lead to life-long consequences. Adults know this because of experience. Remember adolescents lack experience in these new-found bodies and thought processes. Add to this the fact that another characteristic of adolescence is an invincibility theory; they don't believe *bad things* can happen to them! Nature is profoundly wise in offering the means psychologically that young people will not be afraid to experiment in order to be able to build their theories. Consequently, they know intellectually that sex leads to pregnancy, drunk driving leads to accidents, but they believe it won't happen to them!

Am I suggesting that teenagers should go out and experiment in every avenue of life? Of course not, but how does one provide an environment of possibility of exploration during this critical time? Young people will experiment to some degree. The degree depends on two factors: one is temperament and the other is the type of parenting and support they had growing up and have now as they move into a new developmental stage of adolescence.

RESPECTING YOUR TEENS SEARCH FOR IDENTITY

When my child says to me, "I don't know why I have to go to church. The people next door don't go to church, and they are good people." What is our response? If the child were a ten-year-old it might be enough to say, "Our family goes to church because we believe in God and value our church friends and community." This will not be enough for the teenager. The young person realizes with their hypothetical thought ability that there are many ways of being in the world, in regards to religion and God, and everything else for that matter. They know what their parents think, but they need to see what else is out there to build their own theory. Therefore, to tell our adolescent, "Too bad, as long as you live in my house you are going to church," is not enough. They can't build a decent theory on that. We accept their need to know, to explore.

We might say, "You're right. I know a lot of good people who don't go to church. Why don't you ask the next door neighbor about why they don't go and see what they say?" You are respecting your young person's stage of development, their need and right to develop theories. You can also say what you believe. It calls on you to explain your belief system in an honest, specific, and complete manner, such as, "I go to church because it provides a community of like-minded people who are trying to raise their children with moral values. I feel closer to God, etc." Whatever you ACTUALLY believe! I used to say to my children, "What I know so far..." or "What I think so far is."

In this way I acknowledge that I don't own the whole truth either, but that I am a seeker on the planet too. If we come across as if we have all the answers, we leave no space for our child to explore their theories as they are developing. Even though you may not agree with their beginning theories, you support their right to develop their own way of being in the world. You also open the possibility of real communication with your child. You want to be a person with whom they can explore their ideas as opposed to having them depend on other fourteen-year-olds alone to test their theories. If you accept and respect where they are, you open up the possibility of helping them to build a solid theory based on real knowledge from many people who DO have the experience they lack. Our stance should be, "Yes, go ask." Talk to people, maybe even suggest some people like grandparents or coaches that you know or neighbors or friends with differing views and ideas. The worst thing you can do is say, "Don't explore. I'll tell you what to do and think." This leads to a rebellion or worse—a reactionary position. ("If you say it's black, I'll say it is white, just to be opposite from you.") Check out the world; a reactionary stance usually spells violence!

While reading a memoir by Kathleen Norris*, I came upon another instance of the developmental stage of an adolescent being articulated in the actions of some teenagers at a poetry reading. Many of their questions of the poet were not about the poetry itself but concerned identity. How do you know you're a poet? How did you become one? The questions centered on the query of how one becomes who they are. How can you even tell you are something? This line of questioning is part of the contemplation of a teenager.

How do you know if you are gay? How do you know that there is a God? How do you know when you are a writer, a dancer, a worthy person? How did you know what you wanted to do with your life?

Looking back on one's life as an adult, we often feel as if we just fell into things or that one thing led to another. First you just write a poem, then you write another, and then you can't help it; you just write, and then you care to get better at writing poems and you work at it and develop. One day someone else likes your poetry. Even later you are published, but still if someone said you were a poet, you might act surprised. Another day someone asks you what you do, and you say, "I'm a poet." It feels awkward, but you have just articulated what is already true about you. Identity takes time. Maybe teenagers need to know that many of their theories about themselves will form fast and furiously, but most ways of becoming oneself take time, a little steeping like a fine tea.

This alone may come as some relief to an adolescent, but still what can we do to support this identity process?

One of my lovely experiences as a college instructor has been for young people to tell me they want to be a teacher just like me. I'm too embarrassed to ask, "What exactly do I do that you would like to incorporate into your own life?" Sometimes, of course, they do say things they appreciated if they write me a note or email. I might tell them I think it is worth noting very specifically what they like about each teacher they have and what they don't like, and then deciding what it takes to emulate these qualities.

This is true of all qualities we admire in others. Helping young people clearly state what they want, what they like, and how they want to be can be such an asset when they are beginning this process of adult identity.

When I was in seventh grade, I remember looking at the eighth grade girls. I wanted to be like the popular ones. At the time, they wore their sweaters dropping off their shoulders. I did the same. In the teen years of identity formation, you are often looking at the outside of others and copying what you think makes you fit in or be popular. During the process of identity, you figure out how to fit in and then learn that you can decide when and how and if you fit in. The power is within you and not necessarily something only on the outside. It's a process.

Periodically I follow a young man who is walking with a swagger with a tough look on his face. I want to stop him and say, "It's not the walk son. The walk does not make a man."

How will he find out what does make a man? He wants to know, believe me. He wants to be someone who matters.

Wouldn't that be an interesting discussion with young people? What does it mean to be a man or a woman? Gender identity is one part of identity formation. They now need to form a complex, abstract theory of gender.

In my niece's small town in Northern California, when a young girl reaches puberty, a group of women gather with her to affirm her and tell stories and to celebrate this rite of passage. Like Native people before them, these women want to give the girl a blessing and a hope. You are becoming a woman and here are some of the values we place on our womanhood. It is another positive recognition that this adolescent becoming a woman is normal, important, and cause for acknowledgment.

The Virgin of Bennington, by Kathleen Norris

TALK TO ME — SOCIAL EMOTIONAL DEVELOPMENT

At one poignant moment in my daughter's teenage years, through her tears, she said, "Mom, I just want the inside of me and the outside to match." I felt such empathy for her. What could I say but, "Me too?" I could tell her that this is a life-long journey. I could reassure her that it doesn't happen all at once. I could let her know that this is normal angst for a person who is in the throes of the first phase of adult identity formation, but what I thought was, *she is so right on.* She had explained the teenage dilemma of identity, perfectly, and had discovered a truism of the examined life.

Since teenagers are now asking the big questions, they are also experiencing for the first time the human wondering around these questions of self and its relationship to a vast universe. In a way, as each of my children moved to this stage, I felt a sense of empathy for their true loss of innocence. They can never go back to *Never-never land.* It is an exciting adventure to discover who you are, poised on the edge of adulthood, but this statement is from one who is looking backward. When you are new to this feat, you often feel like you are out on the edge of a cliff, and no one has ever been on this cliff or experienced this confusion. The choices are endless, in a way.

You don't know where to begin, and you have no idea that it is normal and the beginning of something instead of the end.

Teenagers are experiencing this whether they articulate it as my daughter did or not. If you asked them directly about it, they might even possibly say that no, they don't worry about who they are; they don't think about it, but in fact, this is their internal work. Often teenagers don't have the words. It isn't that they are hiding. They just don't yet know how to talk about their internal process because it is so new.

This is where sometimes it helps to lay out a few possibilities, as in: *some people have told me they have experienced this,* or *I knew someone who did this or felt that.* The adult needs to forge the river and bring the lifeboat, and model at least some possibilities for crossing the stream.

How do we support this process, reassure them, without infringing on their unique unfolding?

In the formal operational thought stage that teenagers have backed into without their consent, the new hypothetical and analytical processes prepare them to look outside to the bigger world to explore possibilities outside of their experience. In most cases we want to shoo them toward others, and theories other than our own. As family members, though, we can help them to develop frameworks that facilitate organizing processes that aid in understanding how one handles certain dilemmas.

Many older people have read Elisabeth Kübler-Ross's' *Stages of Grief.* This is an example of a framework that grieving people can access to identify their own feelings and to give them a sense that what they are experiencing, others have experienced too. We can check in with the stages, and they give us a sense of joining others in a human way of experiencing the loss of a loved one. It feels supportive without telling us how we should feel. It just offers a list of possibilities that other people have experienced. By talking through our processes of decision making or ways to look at issues from people we have known or from our own experience, we can provide options to an otherwise seemingly endless (to the teenager) array of possibilities.

Stories provide a scaffold of ways humans have maneuvered through the feelings and conundrums of this stage of development or the theory building taking place through the formation of this adult identity stage.

What this cannot be is advice or a telling of our perfect handling of a past similar event. These two forms of telling stunt the growth of the emerging teen. You can expect, as you should, a rolling of the eyes as in the proverbial tale of walking ten miles through the snow, uphill both ways, when I was your age, just to get an education, which I fully appreciated. What is conveyed here is that *you are doing it wrong,* when in fact remember what they need is *you are right where you are supposed to be.*

The *how* of the story and the intention of the story need to be with the purpose of offering one or more possibilities, and only possibilities, that the young person can take or leave.

STRATEGIES TO HELP

Examples of this dialogue might look like this:

- "I remember getting drunk a couple of times, but one time I was drinking wine and eating cheese and apples with friends. I got so drunk I was over the toilet for quite a while, feeling horrible. I couldn't eat cheese and apples together for many years. That day, I just remember knowing I never wanted to make myself sick like that again, and that was the last time."

- Once when my daughter was about fifteen, we were on a hike. As people moved up and down the mountain, I would engage them in conversation. With a sigh, my introverted, quiet daughter said, "You always know what to say to everyone, Mom." I said, "First of all, I didn't when I was your age, but now I just use a formula if I feel uncomfortable or don't know what to say to someone. I either ask them a question about themselves or I tell something about myself. I kind of look at the person and assess what we might have in common and ask a question depending on their age, or how they look or something they have said. So for example, I might say if they look in shape, 'I'm a runner; do you do something to stay in shape?' Or I might say, 'I saw a great movie the other day.' And tell a little about it hoping they might continue to talk about movies. If not, I might ask them, "What type of movies do you like?'"

- When I was in a Shakey's Pizza Parlor attending a soccer event for my daughter when she was about thirteen, I felt a little awkward because I didn't really know any of the parents there. My daughter, of course, was off talking with her friends. I happened to be seated next to the 16-year-old sister of one of the other girls. I turned to her after a while and said, "I feel kind of awkward and out of it because I don't really know anybody here." With relief she looked right at me and said, "Me either," and we talked the rest of the evening. When I told her something about myself, in this case how I was feeling, all of a sudden, we were relating as people, not a young person and a middle-aged person.

Frameworks are ways to hook our life onto theory, and then use this information to integrate our experience into our ever-developing, changing view of the world and our action in the world. Sometimes a framework is something we visit periodically; sometimes it is something needed every day, like an AA meeting for a recovering alcoholic. A framework can be like a hand to hold, or a visit with a familiar friend, or a place to jump from into our one precious life.

MIRROR, MIRROR ON THE WALL, AM I NORMAL?

While reading a provocative novel by Sebastian Barry, I came across this description by the fourteen-year-old girl protagonist that expresses thoughtfully what it is like to be a teenager.

"A fourteen-year-old girl is always vividly aware of her appearance, or thinks she must be, or whatever it is; but speaking of mirrors, I was at the time a slave to one in my mother's bedroom, not because I thought I looked well, but because I did not know how I looked, and labored many a minute to adjust myself into a picture I could trust, or was content with, and never could achieve it. The gold of my hair looked like some wet grass gone wild to me, and for the life of me I did not know the soul of the person that peered back at me in my mother's mossy little mirror." ~ From *The Secret Scripture* by Sebastian Barry

Do you see she doesn't know how she looks? She doesn't know herself yet or her own soul. She is cognizant of the fact she doesn't and clearly longs to have this knowledge. An unfamiliar longing necessary but uncomfortable in its newness, a need to know how I appear, a need to know who I am—this is the trajectory of all adolescents even though they unwillingly boarded the rocket.

Unfortunately, these feelings cause them to judge themselves harshly, to feel perhaps they don't measure up, to feel even something is wrong with them, that they are flawed. In becoming an adult, we know it's true; we are flawed, but not in all ways and we are not alone. I periodically tell my students, "Bottom line, we are ALL messed up, everyone." They always laugh, but the tone of the room totally relaxes, and people visibly sigh. It's a relief to know that an adult can accept this reality, and it gives them a freedom to then be what they can be, to use what they do have, even their flaws.

How do we help move young people then to this acceptance? Why do we want to? Being lost in this new feeling can overwhelm a teenager, and therefore we see things like teens committing suicide for what adults would consider *smaller things*.

Pretend you are looking over the shoulder of this girl into the mirror. What would you say? I might say, "Of course you want people to think you are pretty. What do you see on your face that you like? What I see is (and list the lovely parts.)" "Your soul, what a profound thought you are having. You will now be discovering who you are more and more, but it is a life-long journey. Really, it is a beautiful question to spend a lifetime answering. What would you like your soul to be like?"

Of course, this child would not be saying these things out loud, but I want you to understand and empathize with them that this is what is happening within each of them. Do you see how disconcerting this feels, especially when it is so new? A ten-year-old is not thinking these things.

By pointing out qualities we see, by acknowledging to them that these thoughts are normal, by celebrating this new passage and not fighting it, we give them hope and the freedom to explore and not get stuck in the discomfort.

Of course, many times we shy away from discomfort, but I have heard it said and believe it to be true, that just because something is uncomfortable doesn't make it the wrong thing to do. Think of muscles as you begin an exercise program; think of tests you may have from the doctor to prevent future problems; think of saying "I'm sorry." Think of communicating this way with your child. They may be uncomfortable, especially at first, but the benefits are worth the effort. I know everything in you wants to do what is best for your child to help them grow to be exceptionally *them*. Give it a try. Some people have told me, "Well, you never know how a kid will turn out," as if it is a crap shoot in Las Vegas. This is patently untrue. When you have communication and understanding of the development of your child, when you learn how to be responsive to your child, it can be guaranteed you will have a better outcome.

III

Message #1 —
I Like You

I LIKE YOU

Thrown into a world of upheaval internally and externally, and receiving so much negative feedback, what does a teenager need from the folks in their balcony, the people in fact who need to be the ones cheering them on?

Three messages are vital for the teenager to maneuver most successfully through the adolescent minefield. In other words, if you want to help instead of hinder, their trajectory to adulthood, this is what they need to feel and experience from you:

Message #1: **I like you.** Teenagers might hear, "I love you" from their family, but at this age this isn't enough. You might hear from a teenager, "Yeah, I know my parents love me, but…"

The *but* is all the ways we don't help them to feel that we actually like who they are becoming. They are pulling away from us, and our tendency is to pull away from them. They tap into our own insecurity, and we might feel; *Fine then, you treat me with disdain and don't want to be around me, I don't want to be around you either!* We turn right back into a snotty teenager ourselves, yet we are supposed to be the mature one, the one aiding our child into adulthood. If you don't currently have teenagers, you probably are saying, "I would never do that." But it is an extremely common response to young people. We may not say it out loud but internally we feel it, and consequently, they feel it. Look beyond my exact scenarios to an allowing of the child to retreat and pulling back a little ourselves.

On a trip to spend time with my brother recently, we were talking about our parents who have been deceased for many years. At the end, and quite casually, but with a slight catch in his voice, my brother said, "I know Mom loved me, but I don't think she liked me very much."

The young person needs the opposite. They need our **pursuit!** "I want to be with you. When can we go get a Frappuccino at Starbucks?" "Mom, I'm busy" or "I don't know." We don't let it go. We pursue. "I know, but when can we go? I want to be with you." All the time your child might be rolling their eyes or saying how busy they are. Your job is to make sure that they feel as if they are someone likable.

I love you is not enough. The message is, *I'm crazy about you! You are such a great person to be with. I cherish you.*

Once at a workshop I attended, the presenter said, "If I brought in a Stradivarius violin, all of you would be saying, 'Ahh' with drawn-in breath. Shouldn't we be doing that to those we love? Isn't a person more precious than the most beautiful, valuable instrument?"

This is the message we need to give: "I see you, child, Ahh, (with drawn-in breath). You are someone I cherish, not because you are my child, but because you are turning into such an interesting person, someone very worth being with." Cherishing someone is different than love. It is more an action of love. The VALUE of cherishing is what we need to communicate to our teenager.

How does one show this cherishing? One way, besides pursuing them, is to show them kindness. With our children, our communication, especially as they grow, is often demands, or checking up to see if they are doing what we think they should be doing. Of course, parents need to monitor their children, but this should not be the only form of communication. Usually by this age they know what you expect of them. They know their responsibilities, and we are often just sounding more as if we are nagging them. You have taught most of your lessons by this age. Anyone else you know that you care about who was going through a bad time would probably be the recipient of your kindness. Believe me, they are going through a difficult developmental time in all aspects of their being! It is time now periodically, just to be unflinchingly kind, expecting nothing in return. "I did the dishes for you even though it's your night because I know how much you have to do at school." "I bought you this candy bar or movie pass because I was thinking of you today, and I know 'X' movie opens this weekend."

EMOTIONAL IMMUNIZATION

Before my teenagers would go off to high school, (not in front of their friends), I would grab them and hug them and fuss over them, "Oh, all the girls at that school must just think you are the cutest thing they've ever seen." You can be as corny and dramatic as you like, giving them affection and praise. I considered this an inoculation against going out into a world where eighty percent of the messages directed toward them would be negative. What is your child doing while you do this? They are saying, "Oh Mom," and pulling away a little and acting like you are ridiculous. That's their job; that's normal as they are beginning to try to make their way in the world, but your job is to continue to pursue and be affectionate, even if it is somewhat rejected. Be brave for them; they need it! Even though they will not thank you now, you will absolutely be giving them the underpinning they need to traverse these troubled waters to adulthood.

I'M CRAZY ABOUT YOU— TRUE PRESENCE

My two-year-old grandson is teaching me how to be a grandma. He is also reminding me how to be a person of love. His lessons apply very directly to loving a teenager. The similarities between the social-emotional dilemmas of the two-year-old and the teenager have been duly noted by psychologists.

The two-year-old is involved in his first foray into identity. Erikson describes this as the fight between autonomy and shame and doubt. Autonomy, independence, *me do it*—these are the developmental pushes of a two-year-old that we need to support for their later psychological health. Perhaps then, one might think, let him be, just like a teen. Get out of his way; he doesn't want me there anyway. But the message both two-year-olds and teens need is, "I'm crazy about you. I like you."

But what I have been noticing about my little guy is that he wants me to validate his experience in a sense by being present to it. He says, "Grandma, this way; sit down." He wants me to sit where he wants me and play with him in a way directed by him. He wants my focus to be on what he is doing and what he thinks is important. I DO love him like crazy, but even so, sometimes it is boring to pay attention to what a two-year-old thinks is important, or what a teenager thinks is important. And yet, some of this focus must be felt, must be received for the toddler or teen to move forward. Twenty-four hours a day are not necessary, but some time is necessary. I have read that the average child in the United States receives six minutes a day of attention from their dad. Is that enough?

The dramatic difference between a two-year-old and a teenager in this story, of course, is that a teenager will NOT be asking you to sit down and pay attention to them. Au contraire! The self-consciousness of an adolescent is not a part of the two-year-old experience of growing into oneself.

But what my grandson is saying to me is, "This is the way I can grow and thrive. Your attention to who I am and what I like and accepting those preferences help me know I'm on the right track. My choices are valuable, what I like is valuable, and I am valuable." Remember, he is directing the play, not me! As with a teenager, our job is not to direct the course of their lives, not to choose everything for them when they need to choose to grow, but to be a witness to those choices, those steps to forming the *Who am I?*. A doula is one who supports the birth process but is definitely not giving birth.

When you were young, and your mom or dad came to the play you were in or the soccer game, maybe you just grew up expecting that kind of observance, that kind of witness to your involvements. If you want to know how it feels not to have that focus, speak with someone who never had anyone come to events they were involved in. It was a feeling of being unloved, not cared for, and not cherished.

The last thing a teenager wants is for you to be blasting their music in your bedroom or dressing like them; but they do need a quiet, supportive witness to the events they have decided they need in their lives. It's the willingness or interest to watch, not how loud you scream.

The paying attention to a teenager, this cherishing, how do we make it work?

Your sixteen-year-old comes home with a tattoo across their forearm, or an ear lobe extender. They had never discussed it with you. How do you maintain a relationship of cherishing? Depending, of course, on your real feelings, you have two ways to go that will still maintain support for your child. And of course, there is always the one reaction that could be harmful to their growth.

This tattoo has meaning to your child. There is a reason they got it, and there is probably a reason they didn't tell you about it. What choice do you have? It's a done deal? You have a choice in your reaction, to be a healthy role-model, an adult, or to act as if this is totally about you.

If in fact you are really appalled and shocked, and having a difficult time breathing, then of course you explain your real feelings, right then, right now. You tell your child whatever you are feeling. Example: "I'm shocked. I don't know what to say. Your sweet little body that I brought into this world has these permanent marks and I feel kind of sad, like I've lost my little girl. I know it is your life, but I'm having trouble with this and it is such a surprise. I'm hurt because we didn't talk about it before, as if maybe you don't trust me."

If in fact you are not shocked even though it's not what you would choose, or if you are more aware and in control right this second about your reaction, then it would be best to think of being a witness to their choice. In some ways the tattoo is a fairly dramatic choice, involving a very intimate part of them, their own body. It is a statement about who they are. Example: "Wow, I didn't know you were going to do that. Let me see." Comment on what you find likable or interesting about the actual tattoo, their choice. Maybe you ask them then to tell you what they liked about it. You just show interest in their choice, realizing you are just an observer of their growing identity, and this is one stepping stone where they have chosen to declare their own life, their own preferences.

You don't need to tell them about how you feel about tattoos in general because I would venture to guess they already know. That time is over. The time when you tell all about your biases and preferences in small ways is over. You can tell how you feel if you stick to the "I feel" mode of expression, but your ideas about tattoos are not necessary now. They have made THEIR declaration.

RESPONSIVENESS

In parenting the first task really is to make sure you provide the necessary circumstances for secure attachment to happen in the days and weeks after your baby has been born. The provision for this is meeting the baby's needs with responsive care. Maybe someone would say that the task is to love your baby, but love is an action word. Responsiveness is what love looks like in relationships, all relationships.

Responsiveness is the key to successfully raising a child who will reach their full potential and add to the world and not take away. Each stage of development requires a slightly different type of responsiveness. It is this meeting the child where they are, for who they are, supporting who they are becoming that leads to psychological health and an ability to be a productive member of society ready to give what they have developed, to add to life, to be competent at being a person.

Responsiveness is seeing this person, your child, as unique. He may be similar to you and similar to other humans but *never before on the planet never again. There is no one like him.* For instance, what is your favorite color? Why? Was that learned? I doubt it. It probably is not the favorite color of everyone else in your family. There is no explaining it but to say, you came into the world with certain preferences. I know there are certain foods I will not put it my mouth that other people seem to enjoy. Where did I get those preferences? They are uniquely mine. I am me and no other exact copy exists. So responsiveness is partly this awareness that even as a baby you have your own way of being, your own preferences, your own desires, your own needs, and amount of need. This unfolding of a person, as we watch and guide, is the witnessing privilege of the parent. To be responsive is to get to know the person and to respond to them accordingly. It is to make your family's favorite dinner for them. It is to play with your baby when they give you eye contact and move around and to stop when they keep turning away. It is to read the signals of a person and respond respectfully.

As the child moves to the teenage years, what does responsiveness look like? Once a friend of mine, who had never been a parent but taught college, was talking to a student of his he had come upon in the quad. The girl was going to eat a homemade sandwich but was taking out the lettuce and the tomato, ready to dispose of it. In consternation he wondered why you would make a sandwich with items you didn't enjoy and asked her, "Who made your sandwich?" "My mom," she said. "How old are you?" he asked. "Nineteen," she said. "Your mom doesn't know yet what you don't like?"

Now remember, he is not a parent. I know as a mother that *hope springs eternal* in her mother's heart. She is determined to give her child healthy vegetables whether she eats them or not! She believes, I'm sure, that at least she tried! I can relate to this as a mother, but as a responsive person it makes for a funny scenario! This is the opposite of responsive!

When we have knowledge of typical developmental issues, in other words, realities within a person's physical, thinking, and emotional self that are common to all as we go through life, AND we have knowledge of this person, unique, one-of-a-kind, then we can form a solid foundation for responsiveness. Responsiveness promotes closeness, communicates care or love, and helps support the development of a young person. What do you need at this moment, at this juncture, to allow you to grow and flourish? After many years as a parent educator and college professor, I believe that this responsiveness is the key to excellent parenting.

Responsiveness Examples:

1. Your young person expresses an interest in playing the guitar. Do you go out and buy them a $200 guitar? No. Do you say, "Well, we can't afford a guitar or lessons?" No. You tell the child something responsive and honest like, "That sounds like a cool thing to learn. I bet you would be good at guitar since you like music so much. How do you think you could go about learning?" Ask your child. Suggest finding a student at school who plays or asking the music teacher. Just starting out, your child doesn't need a trained teacher;

they just need someone who knows more than they do. You ask around in your family and friends to see if anyone has an old guitar. (You'd be surprised what people have stored away!) You ask the local music store if they rent them for short periods, or inquire at the school. In other words, you try to support their ideas and initiative. If they prove dedicated and practice, then maybe you can find other ways to provide more sophisticated lessons, etc. The message is that their ideas are good; they can follow their interests. You are supporting them and also modeling how to take hold of life and how to empower oneself.

2. Your child has always been interested in animals. They are the child who picks up stray dogs and saves fallen birds and tries to nurse them back to health. They are not asking anything of you, but you know their interests because you know them. When they are a teen, you contact your local zoo or animal shelter and investigate volunteer opportunities or classes that support this interest and offer them to your child for a summer involvement. This is responsive.

3. When your child comes home from school all sullen and sad looking you say, "It is so hard to be in high school. Ask any adult; it will not be their favorite time of their life!" You are responding to what you see or feel your child might be feeling based on typical teenagers and on how your child generally behaves. This is responsive. Don't ask, "What's wrong?" They will say, "Nothing."

Many times I have said to my own children and to others, "It's hard to be a person." Not trying to fix the feelings of discouragement, etc. but being responsive to what IS, right here, right now.

Doesn't it feel lovely when you say to your partner, "I have a neck ache," and they rub your neck? When you feel like Chinese food and that is where you go for dinner? When you get a promotion and you see genuine happiness for you on their face? When you come home needing a hug and you don't even have to ask? These are responsive acts.

A teenager is in particular need of responsiveness. The difference with teens is that they are often more difficult to read. They often don't know how to express their needs. They sometimes hide because of the internal upheaval, because of their belief that they are the only ones experiencing this depth of feeling, not just now but ever.

MOVE TOWARD

When everything in you wants to pull away, the effort of a parent should be to go toward your teenager. I think the attitude that my friend had is one to cultivate. When his third son reached fourteen, Dave, the dad, told a group of friends, "Well, I'm a dork again." By the third child he realized it was just a phase, or developmental stage that causes teenagers to criticize their parents for how they dress, or what car they drive, or how they speak. By child three, my friend knew it had nothing to do with him. He could make light of it. This attitude would be one to develop as one parents a teen. It's nothing personal; it is short term, and it says everything about the sender and very little about the receiver.

Since our self-esteem is at its lowest ever at thirteen, just as part of the developmental process, we know teens are vulnerable. As you look at history, it seems evident that when one is forced to take a *low* position, one tries to find someone lower than they are in order to have a sense of power. Since a young person is trying to form an identity, the first area of focus is how things look. Very soon they learn through pain, trial, and error that everything is not as it appears. As they glance backward at middle childhood, they see it for what it holds: a more concrete, black-and-white view of the world. This child view has to be put aside, in order to explore the ideas, theories, and attitudes that make up this diverse planet so that they can form their own theories.

A friend recently told me of a father who no longer speaks to his adult children. We were lamenting the sadness of this situation and speculating on the cause. It reminded me of the times I pulled away from my own mother when I was a teenager, disregarding her feelings or what was going on for her. I remember not wanting to hold her hand anymore. I remember listening to what she was saying about something but pretending I didn't care much about what she said.

As a teenager you are on the cusp of finding your own way. You need to strike out on the journey. You are not thinking about whether you are alienating people of your parents' generation but that you are independent and fit in with your own cohorts. Yet you need to know you are cared for and, more importantly, valued for the person you are right now and for the person you are becoming. We don't value a baby any less for acting like a baby and crying for his/her needs and so it should be with adolescents. Accept them where they are. Treat them with acceptance and respect and know they aren't finished yet. Teenagers will do and say things that from another person may be considered hurtful or rude, but the teenager is speaking and acting from a place of protection much of the time.

RELATIONSHIP DEFENSE— INOCULATION

My brother tells the story of a situation from his wayward days as a teen that illustrates the power of relationship. My father got the call, late one night, that my brother had been caught with some buddies stealing hubcaps in the parking lot of Disneyland. At that time, we lived about forty miles from Disneyland. My brother's memory is that our dad picked him up at the police station and didn't say a word as they got into the car. My brother was figuring he would get the anger and lecture of a lifetime. But as they drove wordlessly home, all my big, strong, impatient, logical father did was cry. The memory of my dad's reaction has stayed with him a lifetime. The worst punishment given—my dad's disappointment.

To build a relationship with a child that protects and saves during the teenage years begins much younger. Having clear expectations and good follow-through with lots of communication that values the person but sets limits on the acts is the ticket to building the bond that is all you have left to protect kids when they become teenagers.

To build theories young people experiment. This is all well and good if the experimentation doesn't go too far out of bounds. The fear of disappointing one's parents often keeps the boundaries set a little more safely. In order for this relationship to be most protective, trust must be developed.

Trust is a developed disposition. It comes from interactional proof that a person will be true with you, that they won't judge you or believe badly of you, that they believe that you are worth something.

The first means of learning to be a person comes from others telling us, showing us, and making sure that we do what a human being needs to do to function well. If you have ever changed your behavior because of *the look* from your mom or dad, you know what I am talking about. As a baby, you crawl over to the fireplace and look back to your parent to judge your action from the reaction of their face. If your parent is encouraging and has a positive look, you will continue; but if your parent looks scared or negative, you may crawl back towards her. It is your mama's expression that determines your behavior. At a very real level you need this woman to survive, so you listen to her. Over time she pulls you away or says *no* or does something that you don't like, moves you away from what you wanted, etc. The disapproval on her face is the building block of the relationship you have with her.

Over time you know her likes and dislikes and her facial expressions better than she does. When you bring home a boy, before she says anything, you know if she likes him. When you have a new outfit, you know if she likes it before she says a word. Through the years this knowing her, as she teaches you about the world, allows you to adapt your behavior to fit in to the world, to be a success and have behaviors that you need to survive, but the first means of learning was from the relationship you had with the important attachment figures in your life. When my dad cried, his disappointment was the punishment. It doesn't feel good to have given my dad that much pain. Does this mean I never do what I know my parent won't like? No. But it does mean that my parent's feelings do impact my behavior, especially if I feel valued by them.

Give your child the message, *I trust you.* Even if you feel frightened of what choices they make, you want them to believe you trust them. Remember we don't have to always say what we think. Our job is to help them develop into a productive member of society. Most of our lessons have been taught, but our support and trust, is invaluable.

AFFECTION— A CHERISHING FACTOR

Once while teaching a parenting class to fathers of two-year-olds, the men were talking about their own fathers. They were saying that their fathers had never told them they loved them and were not affectionate. Their point was how different they were as fathers. I, of course, didn't say it out loud but I wanted to say, "You don't remember what your dad did when you were two. He probably held you on his lap and kissed and hugged you. You remember when you were ten on up. Let me see what you do at that time with your own children."

In other words, unfortunately, many parents are affectionate when it's easy to be, when your children throw themselves at you and ask to be held and carried, etc. But as soon as the child grows to be a little more independent, the parent pulls away when the child does not necessarily initiate affection. This often is exacerbated when the teen reaches puberty and the parent may feel more awkward around this changing body and child.

Your child, particularly in the teenage years, still requires affection and touch as we all do. Obviously, at all ages we need to be respectful of other people's bodies. What can happen, especially to girls, is that they may have sex earlier than they really want to just to get the physical attention they can receive. To prevent this and to show our love, we need to continue to be affectionate to teenagers.

I remember a teenager speaking once about how her father, suddenly, would not let her sit on his lap and was physically treating her more remotely than he had right before she reached puberty. Remember, to her, her father is her father and she is his child, so if they have had a close relationship up until this point and he suddenly changes, this will be a confusing message to a person on the cusp of adulthood but still a child. In this regard take the cue from your child. If they still want to sit on your lap, let them. If they don't, then don't initiate it. But continue to hug and kiss your children as you always have, even if they squirm a little. Be respectful but don't pull away.

Obviously, some families are more affectionate than others, but it is a way to show, *I cherish you.* Especially when they are feeling so awkward in their vastly changing body, if we stop being affectionate it might add to their discomfort about the value of their body.

How can we be affectionate? Hugs, back rubs, hair brushing, putting your arm around them while you are watching TV. Continue what you have done before. They will not be asking for it, but they need it! Remember, pursue time with them. Time together is a way we show how much we like someone.

The message is, *I like you. You are someone I like to be around. You are valuable as a person, not just my child.*

A film from West-Ed about the RIE philosophy of Magda Gerber, I have shown in an infant class, taught me a very valuable lesson about hugging. Magda is helping a crawling baby to work his own way out of a semi-stuck position under a table. She lies down on the floor near him and lets him solve his problem with support. After he is out, he is crying and crawls into her lap for comfort. While in her arms, she rubs his back a little and then the lightbulb goes on for me. She holds him, as long as HE needs to be held. When HE has had enough comfort, he crawls down from her lap and begins playing. The lesson for me with my grown children, with anyone really, was that it is responsive to allow other people to hug, as long as THEY would like. I began to notice that I often would break hugs with people, even my own children. A more loving and responsive tact would be to let them decide how much comfort they need. We often try to talk people, small ones, big ones, out of their feelings and needs. We say to the child, "You're fine," when they are crying. We tell people to move on when we are uncomfortable with their feelings. Better, just acknowledge their feelings; best, allow them to feel their feelings and I guarantee they will move on. If we continue to tell others not to feel what they are feeling, it will be more difficult for them to move on.

PURSUE WITHOUT SPOILING— WANTS AND NEEDS AND THE WISDOM TO KNOW THE DIFFERENCE

Of course, we need to listen to our child, but beware. Sometimes in their need for power or in their fear of having their lives taken over by us, or in their embarrassment to remain cool, they push us away. Your child might say, "You don't need to come to my game," or even, "you don't have to come to my graduation."

Pursuit is a beautiful, affirming stance. "I really want to come. I like watching you play. I want to be there." Or maybe even more appropriate, just assume, obviously, family supports each other. Don't ask *them* if you should come. When we ask, often this implies WE are not sure we should be there.

What is lovelier than when someone makes an effort for you, not with pressure or an agenda but with the message: *You are important. You are worth the effort.*

Love is action. My dad always used to thank my mom for making dinner. Did he have to? That was a part of her job as they had defined their roles, but how loving to continue to let her know he appreciated her effort.

My cousins always come outside and wave to us when we leave their home, even if they have other people still in their home. The act feels very loving. It makes us feel that we are worth their time and effort. Of course, we could say to them, "Oh you don't have to." But it feels good to have been shown that act of love.

Our teenagers are vulnerable. They are not sure of themselves, by definition. Love is never wasted.

It often comes up in my classes, "Can you spoil a child?" Yes, but not by showing them love. If you give a child everything they WANT, yes, they can be spoiled. Often people mistake giving children material things as love, but this will never match up to time, appreciation, and focused attention.

Sometimes parents give children what they want because they think they will be loved if they do this. Naturally, we want our children to love us and like us. The best way to build love and regard is through respect and acceptance. Through the three messages you will build a relationship that will last through time.

Acceptance does not mean letting them do whatever they want; this is another misconception. We need to accept that they are in a particular stage of life. It is not like any other. In a sense they need the same type of all-in we gave to them as a baby. They couldn't tell us their needs then, and often at this age they cannot express what is going on. In understanding the stage, we have the opportunity to help them find what they can utilize from the outside world.

When the imperative is to find an identity, to fit in, and to be like a grownup, teenagers often need to pretend that they know what is happening when they can't possibly know. Often people say, "Oh today kids know all about sex already as teenagers because of the internet." My contention is that they know all the words, but nations have been won and lost over sex. I'm an older person and I can't possibly claim to know all the intricacies and depths of sex. There is no way a thirteen, fourteen, fifteen, or sixteen-year-old knows all about sex, even if they are sexually active. To know takes time and experience, information. They have the clinical, physical information but not the subtle, human, relationship, complexity of sex, or any other endeavor for that matter. The difference, because of their formal operational thought, described by Piaget, is they are capable of understanding. In other words, don't underestimate them, but truly it is also detrimental to overestimate their knowledge and abilities.

Overestimating leads to a more hands-off policy. Either *I'll let them figure things out for themselves* or *I'll keep my distance* because *they think they know everything already.* The difficulty with teenagers often is that they don't act like they want our support. Despite this, we can make their life easier and their theories for their life more cohesive.

As the consequences become more frightening for the parents, they often try to restrict their child to make sure nothing happens to them, understandable from a parent's point of view and sometimes necessary, but not your most important tool. You cannot protect a teenager from everything. They will see images and hear words that you were not exposed to as a child. The tools that are the most useful in this regard are communication and relationship. By continuing to listen to them, then we have the right in their eyes to speak also.

Teenagers will rarely ask questions about important ideas they are thinking or worrying about. They are afraid to seem vulnerable and *non-grown-up*. They are reluctant to hear the lecture on what they should think. But clearly, they do have many questions. Don't be daunted by their reactions; forge ahead. Bring up topics you know teenagers are building theories about.

For example, "I know you know a lot about sex and we've talked, but I've been thinking about this, and I just wanted to say it, even though it's an uncomfortable topic." You might say, "Sometimes sex can be a way someone uses a person and therefore it can be disrespectful." You may use a story from your own life or something you read that made you think of this topic.

The important message is to let them know you like them as a person, not just as your child. As a matter of fact, you are delighting in this new adolescent with all they bring to you and your family. Don't back away but move toward them with responsiveness to this emerging adult.

IV

Message #2—
I Accept You

AMBIVALENT IDENTITIES (I ACCEPT YOU)

On the very same day at different times in interactions with my son when he was a teenager (about seventeen), this is what he said, "Mom, I'm just a kid," and later, on the same day, "You know I'm grown up and can make my own decisions." What is a parent to believe? How does it feel to be so torn within oneself? Are they both true? How do I help my child maneuver between these two realities?

When I was a teenager (about eighteen), I remember going for a walk with my mom around our neighborhood. She was talking to me about my dad in a woman-to-woman way. She expressed some of her real feelings about my dad's drinking. I clearly remember having two distinct feelings. I was proud and pleased that she was sharing with me as a friend and woman, and I also wanted to say, "But I'm just your kid. I'm not sure I want to know."

Now that I have an adult daughter, I understand better this process of transition between parent and child as they grow into adults. But my feelings at the time reflect a teenage dilemma, if you are lucky enough to still be under a parent's wing. This feeling of being caught between childhood and adulthood is a very legitimate concern.

In many cultures and certainly in the past in all parts of the world, you were a grown-up in the teen years. After all, your body can produce offspring, and you have needs for independence. In our culture today, though, it is very difficult for a teenager to survive on their own. Mainly because of economic concerns and the amount of time and schooling necessary to have a good paying job, adulthood has been postponed, in a sense, in our day. Probably, too, the fact that people are generally living longer and in many families, don't need to support themselves, are factors in the prolonging of adolescence which has been documented in our culture.

This is the plight of the teenager as they move toward identity. How are we to support these conflicting feelings?

I never pointed out to my son that he had said these two things in one day. I held it in my heart with tenderness. My mom did the right thing. The young teens themselves must bridge the worlds of childhood and adulthood. The parent recognizes their readiness to be more of an adult and treats them accordingly. In this treatment and recognition, the child sees a reflection of their own readiness and capability. *Mom thinks I can handle it; I guess I can or at least I'll try.*

If I say things like, "See, you're just a child;" "You don't make good decisions," or "You are a self-centered child," they will have no support of their emerging adult self and will tend to fulfill your expectations that they are still a child. This is another case of *what I see in you.* This is another aspect of faith. A tuned-in parent sees the budding adult and begins to reflect that to the young person.

In high school, I went to an all-girls Catholic school. It was generally a wonderful place of support; but in the late 60's at least, they had many rules that began to seem inane and ridiculous to me. I remember complaining to one of the nuns in my senior year. I very confidently proclaimed how archaic and ridiculous some of these rules were. She said to me in a calm voice, "You're ready to move on." I viewed it as a huge compliment that she saw me as more adult now, ready to manage an adult way of being. I never forgot this reflection she gave me of myself. If she hadn't seen what was already there, she could have missed an opportunity to support my identity, my adult self. She could have given me a lecture on school rules, or discipline or some such, but she saw what was already there and pointed it out to me. She gave me hope in my ability to cross the bridge successfully.

Throughout time, the social animals that we are have required a care and mentoring in how to grow, how to be a person. The teenager has the ability cognitively to manage the type of processes needed to launch, but what of the processes.

When I moved out of my childhood home into an apartment by myself, after about two months I told a friend, "I feel nervous. I'm not sure I can do this." I always will remember that she said, "You're doing it." It was such an affirmation and reminder to me. Be nervous if you want, but you have been proving you can do it. The feeling she reflected back to me was just what a teenager needs to hear. In one way or another we need to communicate our confidence in their ability to handle their own life, to be an adult.

When you are young you still think that others might be very different from you. They don't really know yet that we are all faking it, so to speak. Momentary magic happens in life periodically, but most of it just builds over time and each little step adds up to something that may look like a big leap. We need to tell them that we didn't just emerge as an adult but had insecure feelings of non-readiness too.

DECISION MAKING

Over the years I have hiked with a friend who has walked to mountain peaks all over the world. When I began to hike with him, I was a runner. I would always ask him how far we were going to hike. He would tell me, "That is a runner's question. Hiking is not about distance as much as it is about how many vertical feet you will climb and at what altitude." As time went by, he would ask people along to hike who seemingly were in good shape from some other physical activity. As they would struggle along, he would tell me, "The best preparation for hiking is hiking."

The best preparation for life is to practice, when young, decision-making and problem-solving. One way to think of life, although it sounds somewhat negative, is that it is just one problem to solve after another. In the US today, we have begun to rob our children of the opportunity to solve problems and make meaningful decisions. We have taken protection of our children to new heights. Perhaps as a result of misunderstandings of the meaning of the self-esteem movement of the 70"s and further exacerbated by fear of litigation, we have removed challenges almost systematically from the lives of young people.

In the 50's, 60's and 70's when I was being raised, children were allowed to maneuver throughout their neighborhoods, essentially unsupervised, until the street lights came on. During these forays of childhood, you learned to deal with the myriad personalities of adults and children in your neighborhood. You learned what was safe and unsafe from experience and childhood sharing. You learned what houses, yards, and dogs to avoid. You developed intuitions from interactions that were not overseen by an adult. The actions of childhood were the teacher. You got teased, ostracized, put down, fought with, and learned to be a part of a group all through the experiential learning of the streets.

As children come from homes where everyone works, they are either told to stay in their home for safety sake or they are in some type of supervised group care. If I tease you and I am overheard by an adult, generally the adult will solve the problem for the children so the children on both sides of the equation are robbed of the opportunity to learn about themselves, about others, negotiation and problem solving skills, and the confidence that only comes with having an impact in the world, all by yourself. Skills are learned. Working with others, communication, decision making, problem solving, and negotiation are all learned skills. They don't come from just being told or just watching but from the critical element of practicing.

How then, in this insulated, protected time of childhood and growing, can children practice these necessary activities?

I once heard it said that you should never do for a child what they can do for themselves. I am fully aware that this is a cultural construct of the larger U.S. culture that values independence, but this is where I am coming from. The idea is solid of course. If you want a child to be confident to do things on their own, they need to practice. In the United States twenty-seven percent of individuals live on their own. At some time in most people's lives, they will live alone, forced or chosen, and they need to be able to make decisions. One of the skills listed as one the world needs and looks for in its current workers is the ability to make decisions.

Studies done after the Depression about the effects this historical period had on children of various ages revealed that children who were very young in their families as they lost work and the ability to have what they needed did not fare as well in their future. They were less likely to be productive citizens than children who were older at the time. Children from about ten on were actually needed by their families to help with bringing in money or tending the vegetables if they were so lucky to have a garden. The researchers believed that older children, through these experiences, learned skills that served them in later life. They knew they were truly needed for the survival of the family. They were not just given a chore like feeding the dog so that they would learn responsibility, but they were vital and they felt it. One can see that this testing in the world, perhaps selling newspapers or delivering groceries on your bike, gave them the opportunity to make decisions independently as they faced the real world. Does this remind you of the movie, "It's a Wonderful Life"? George, the young protagonist, saves someone's life by intervening with the intoxicated pharmacist who has incorrectly filled a prescription. George is the delivery boy for the pharmacist; he was just a kid.

With a two-year-old, we begin the practice of decision-making by giving them choices between things that we approve of as a parent. We say, "Would you like a cheese sandwich for lunch or turkey?" "Would you like an apple or an orange?" "Do you want me to hold your hand in the parking lot or carry you?" We give them options within the scope of the developmental abilities of the child while setting parameters of acceptable behavior. As the child gets to elementary school, they choose their friends and when they do their homework (not if). We ask them for input on family decisions. Maybe we let them choose a dinner for the week and help make it. We ask for ideas on what we might do this weekend as a family. We ask them questions about what they think they should do in certain situations instead of telling them. For example, "Henry is calling me names at school." We listen to the story by using active listening. "That must hurt. I can see you're not happy about that." Then we ask, "What do you think you should do about it?" In other words, this is their life; we don't solve all their problems for them. We are a support system to their lives. We make the final decisions as a parent, but we allow the child to have as much power as possible in making decisions that affect them.

As teenagers, we even up the ante of decision making. I remember a parent of a twelve-year-old in my class who said as she was leaving our Parent Education class, in a casual manner, "I have to go because *we* have a history test tomorrow." This belief robs the child of the opportunity to take responsibility and to make decisions. Your child comes home and tells you, "I have a history test tomorrow." You empathize with their feeling, whatever it may be. Then you say, "Is there something I can help you with to study for your test?" It is their test. You can act as a support, but it is their decision at twelve whether they need your help.

MONITORING

Monitoring is our job and research has shown that adolescents need and thrive with monitoring. Observation and communication about time spent, where and when and with who, are all part of monitoring. As a parent you have standards, and you make sure there is follow-through to meet those standards.

HONESTY—THEY CAN TAKE IT!

Now that your teenager is in formal operational thought, you can tell your child about your life. You can use your own youthful stories and mishaps to share information with them at opportune times when it is NOT in the guise of "You better do this, or you better not do that."

Many people hesitate to use their own failures or lessons from their teenage years because they think it is giving their child permission to screw up. I believe it has the opposite effect. Just as research shows that the more information a young person has about sexuality, the longer they delay sexual activity. The more real-life lessons that young people hear, the more usable the information is in their own decision-making. Sharing your life, especially the lessons or failures, often stimulates communication as a side benefit.

Teenagers need to build theories in a few short years about life. They need theories about sex, drugs, vocation, roles, identity, style, spirituality, money, and even death at some level. Through experimentation and honest conversation with elders and peers about how other people have arrived at theories, young people will begin to form set ideas of how the world works and how they want to abide within and interact with it.

During this time, we can share how we arrived at some of our beliefs, but we need to be humble about it and honest and open-minded, not unduly rigid. If you began sexual activity yourself at a young age, you can talk to your child about this. How do you feel about it looking back? Do you regret it? Do you think it was right for you? What were some of the consequences? What chances did you take and how did these play out? Did you have a friend at that time who made different decisions and what were the consequences of their choices? You need to be detailed and reflective and thoughtful as you share.

When my daughter was a freshman in high school, she had a boyfriend for a short time named Seth. Since they couldn't really go out, they used to go to each other's homes. One day when they were at my house, walking by the den I noticed that Seth had his arm around Natalie on the couch. She on the other hand was leaning away from him. When he left, I asked her how she liked him. She told me he wanted to kiss her, and she didn't want to. I listened and then explained that it seemed there could be two reasons she didn't want to kiss him. The first being, of course, that some people you are just not attracted to in that way and you don't want to kiss them. The second reason could be that she was not ready. "I think he's cute, Mom, but I just think I'm not ready." This led to a discussion of what she could do now about that. In other words, the age-old dilemma of the relationship game was her learning edge. How do you let someone know your limits without hurting their feelings? Do you do subtle messages or just tell them clearly what you are feeling? The important point here is that it is not what the young person chooses, but the window into the processes involved in different types of adult thinking. The *apprenticeship in thinki*ng is valuable to introduce a new formal operational thinker to their new and in some ways, scary way of thinking.

If you remember having a two-year-old, one strategy to keep the peace and empower your child was to give them choices. In the very same way, through our honest open processing talk, we are giving them a view into the options for ways to approach their decisions. Adult thinking options are available to the teenage mind; they have just not had practice in utilizing them. As an adult who cares for a teenager, we can sometimes express for them the options, as long as we do it in a way that clearly allows them to be the one who is making the decision. Our faith in their ability to make decisions is the cornerstone of the trust from our end as the adult.

A young man who is a good friend of our family had a tough adolescence in terms of family dynamics. Suffice it to say, his mother had moved away from the area; and his father had set him up in an apartment because his new wife didn't want him to live with them. Consequently, here was a very intelligent young man who didn't have a lot of guidance in terms of his decisions. In his very early adulthood he fell in love with a girl and wanted to create a family with her. I'm sure it's obvious that he wanted to create what he had been missing for a long time. Your heart can easily understand the motivation. But to bring a child into the world and to marry at a young age is a difficult road, especially in today's world. One day when he was talking to me about it, I could feel that this sexual experience was quite eye opening to him and of course quite exciting. I mentioned to him that I hoped he wasn't thinking with his private parts. He laughed. The next day he came back and asked me, "What exactly did you mean when you said that?"

I was struck by the innocence of the question and the fact that we know so little of our own motivations and choices when we are young. Here is a life-changing choice. It may not be ultimately important that he get it right, but it would be helpful to him now and in the future to actually make a decision, not just let passion or ignorance wash him away.

Strategies for teenagers are like money in the bank of life. The strategies associated with decision-making can be intentionally taught to young people.

This gray matter (as in your brain) process can be pulled out as a trusted way to go forward.

DECISION MAKING 101:

1. Write out the dilemma or talk it out with a trusted person. What is the issue to be addressed or solved?

2. List the possible choices without judging or evaluating them.

3. Evaluate each possible choice by making two lists: positive outcomes and negative outcomes of this particular choice.

This is no guarantee that hindsight will prove it was the *right* choice. But a considered choice has several benefits:

a. It is more likely to be one you take responsibility for and

b. It is more likely to fit with your beliefs, ideas, and feelings so you may feel more comfortable with it in the long run. Plus, it offers a way to approach dilemmas that aren't based on knee-jerk emotional reactions.

After I had been teaching college for a few years, I had a lovely, bright young man in my class who mentioned that he had a five-year-old. I was surprised because he was so young. As I got to know him, he revealed that he and his girlfriend had gotten pregnant when he was a senior in high school. He had gone to a prestigious high school in the college neighborhood and had a really loving and great sounding family. Near the end of the semester, I recall a conversation we had. He was sharing with me that even though he loved his wife and son, it had been difficult. He said, "I wish someone would have told me." I just looked at him wide-eyed and he said, "OK, OK they did tell me."

Decision-making is about choices, empowering young people to believe their choices have meaning. Meaning is a portion of the quest of teenagers, and as they make decisions and learn from them, then they feel able and responsible for their own lives.

TELL IT LIKE IT IS — YOUR CHOICES HAVE MEANING

When I was in high school, I'm sure the main reason I didn't have sex was because I would disappoint my parents; and if I got pregnant, they would have been devastated. Looking back that relational control on my behavior was a positive thing. Putting off sexual activity until a little maturity of choice is part of the equation, and in general, it works better for young people.

The important lesson here is that in guiding or disciplining our teenagers, the relationship we have with them is our most powerful enforcer. I have heard it said that by the time a child is twelve, he knows what we think and that in many ways we have nothing left to teach. At this time, we need to shift away from teacher and move to support person. Can teenagers do whatever they want? Do they need monitoring and guidance? Of course, they still need us, but the parenting job is going through a paradigm shift. Our influence mostly comes from the relationship of trust and care we have with our child. Hopefully you have built this through the years by listening to your child even when you put limits on their behavior.

It is time to be a person with this young one. They need to know how their behavior affects us. They need to know our real feelings about what they are doing when we have a concern, but without using shame.

Flying to Hawaii recently, I sat next to a young woman who had three children. We began to talk about parenting, and she started to tell me how differently she was parenting her children than her mother parented her.

One of her stories was one I had heard from other young people. Honestly, much of my motivation for writing this book comes from this story and similar ones.

When she was in high school, her mother would not like how she was dressed and even called her a slut. The young woman told me she didn't even have her first kiss until she was eighteen, so she was not even close to being what her mother called her. You can imagine, or maybe you know the hurt this causes, the many very negative and harmful messages you are giving a person as they are trying to decide who they are. Some young people are told, "You're not leaving this house looking like that!" When we speak to them in this manner, we are not only being somewhat dishonest, but we are depriving them of our true selves and an opportunity to have a positive impact on their behavior. A common outcome of this type of talk is that the child hides their clothes from the parent and takes them somewhere else and changes, so they are essentially lying to the parent. They can't possibly grow into believing their choices have meaning if we attack them in this way. Some of us are appalled by this story, and sadly it is a true story.

What was going on in the mother? Fear. The mother was afraid that her daughter would be cheapened, that she would be hurt perhaps by how she dressed.

What are we really feeling in these circumstances anyway? Perhaps we may feel like this, "When I see you dressed in those clothes, I feel afraid that someone will misinterpret who you are. I feel scared that someone will take advantage of you or they might think you are looking for sex. You are so lovely, and I don't want anyone to hurt you." It could be as simple as, "I love you so much and I don't want anyone to hurt you."

If she could communicate her *feelings* instead of hurtful accusations, she would gain many things. She would become closer to her daughter, her daughter would feel loved, she would be more likely to consider what her mom says, and she would have more information to make decisions about her own behavior. Mom could have turned the negative fear into a positive closeness.

When she called her daughter a slut, on the other hand, she was giving messages of non-trust. She alienated herself from her daughter because she was admitting she didn't really know her. One negative consequence may be that the daughter felt like, *what the heck; my Mom thinks I'm a slut anyway; maybe I should just act like one.* So many people have told me that these were their exact feelings including the young mom on the plane.

To your son wearing clothes that you think make him look like a gang member, you can say, "I am afraid that someone might think you belong to a gang or something when you wear those clothes. I love you so much I don't want anything bad to happen to you."

We can think about our true motivations when we want to criticize a teenager for their choices. I would venture to bet that most of the time we are feeling fear for them because we love them or care for them so much. Say that! Say exactly that! The teenager may not thank you now, but they will be much more likely to listen and to follow what you have said. You are showing respect for them and being an honest communicator. Your true and honest feelings of fear and concern and love and the reasons for them will help young people to make better decisions. They will understand you are on their side, even if they think you are old-fashioned, etc.

When we yell at them out of fear, the meaning becomes lost; and they consequently have no real motivation to change their behavior or to think about what their behavior might mean. They are spending their energy defending themselves and feeling misunderstood.

The relationship you have with them will cause them to act in certain ways more aligned with your feelings. Just as we don't want to hurt or disappoint our children, they even more so do not want to hurt or displease us. One aspect of love is that we accommodate, adapt, and change our behavior for the loved one. This is true in all loving relationships. Since birth our children have been studying us, and they want to do what will keep our relationship intact.

One of the challenges of forming one's identity in the teenage years, Erikson tells us, is to form an identity of oneself that is unique and internally consistent while still maintaining our relationship with our family. We need to become who we are, but without alienating the important people in our lives. If one is attacked, though, for this emerging identity, they will fight back. All people fight back when attacked, or internalize a lack of faith and belief in themselves.

If we alienate our children at this stage, we have lost our connection of support. Remember, they desperately need to have a balcony person applauding them from the sidelines. Parent worries, fears, and attempts to control are often based, oddly enough, on love. Leave the negative way of expressing this behind and practice saying your true feelings behind the fear. Many times, when I was the most worried, I started our conversation, "I love you so much I want all good things for you." Then I can add the, "That's why when I see you coming home drunk, I'm worried something might happen to you that you couldn't change back." The circumstances change but our reaction can be an honest description of our own feelings. "I feel…"

ENABLING TRUST – FAITH

When my son was a senior in high school, prom night was connected to an *after party* at the YMCA which is called Prom Plus. Most of the students choose to go because it is so much fun and free! They have a band and games, such as putting on protective bubble suits and bashing each other with swords, riding each other's shoulders and trying to knock each other onto mats. They have body-size gyroscopes to ride in and food of every imaginable kind that a teenager would want, and all their friends are there.

The rationale of the parents, of course, is to provide a safe place to prevent some of the dangers of prom night, i.e., drinking, pregnancy, drugs, etc.

A few weeks before prom night, the school sent a letter to each parent asking us if we wanted to get a phone call (at 2:00 a.m., mind you) on prom night if our child did not show up. Here was my opportunity to develop one emotional message my young person needed. In front of him, I laughed and crumpled the paper and said, "Isn't this ridiculous? I know I can trust you to do what you tell me you're doing. I don't need to check on you like a young child or something. Isn't this kind of insulting to you guys?" These in fact were my true feelings, but instead of keeping them to myself, it was my chance to show him how much trust I have in him and our relationship. Could he not show up? Yes. Could he go places that he doesn't let me know about? Yes. But, in fact, this is much less likely to happen if he truly believes I trust him. Trust in human relationships, even the most loving ones, is not a given. It is a feeling, yes, but it is based on words and actions over time. Trust begets trustworthiness.

Young people most often get the emotional message that the world believes they are untrustworthy, that they always lie and are doing things they aren't supposed to do. We are poised to say, "See, I know you will screw this up." The sad fact is, we are not hiding this attitude from them. When they are trying to form a *Who am I?* they bring to it the expectations of important others in their life. If they think their parents, teachers, etc., expect them to be a sneak or liar, they can develop an attitude of *so what the heck*.

The emotional message they need is: *Your choices have meaning. I believe that you make sound choices. If you like this music, this boy, these clothes, there must be a meaningful reason that you do.* How can they develop who they are when everyone around them is telling them that their choices are ridiculous, or useless or sometimes even laughable? Remember, all they lack is experience.

It reminds me of a story from a parenting class I once taught for parents and their two-year-old's. A mother came to class on one of the hottest days of the year. She dragged herself in, telling me that she had been battling her two-year-old's tantrums all morning because he wanted to wear his overalls to school. Because it was such a hot day, of course the mom was choosing shorts.

The next day the mom called me and relayed this information. When they had gotten home that day, the child had managed to communicate to his mom that the reason he had wanted to wear overalls was because the slide was so hot, and he wanted to be able to go down the slide! Even two-year-old's choices have meaning! We don't always understand, but the meaning is there in human behavior! The precept is: Behavior is motivated by need.

Our job is to support the MEANING of the choice. How does one do this?

I say to my child, "When I hear that music and I hear the "F" word over and over or I hear some words that make me think they are talking about using women or hurting women, I'm uncomfortable with the music you're listening to. I know if you like it, there must be more to it than that. What do you like about it?"

I remember listening to songs in the 60's that my parents found offensive because they had drug references in them. I was interested in how the music made me feel or that you could dance to it. It wasn't the drug parts I was focusing on.

Through my sincerity, wanting to understand, letting them know, I know, it does have meaning to them, I am supporting their ability to make meaningful choices. A side benefit, of course, is that I increase the likelihood of our communicating again if I am not judgmental. I am also truly understanding another human, who also happens to be my child!

CHOICES

While teaching a class for parents of teenagers, a mother came to me and was sharing that her eighteen-year-old son was telling her about his girlfriend one day. "She is needy and now even her mom is needy," he said, "They want me to help them solve problems. I always seem to pick needy girls." She told me she had used reflective listening to give back to him what he was saying. He was not seemingly that upset by his disclosure, but she had a sense that possibly she had not done enough.

I told her there was just one more thing to ask. "Do you like it?" In other words, do you like that they are needy? In order to aid her son in making real decisions and choices, she can help him not only identify his situation but to make a judgment about his future behavior and choices he has within his life and relationships. If you like being needed and you feel satisfied in this role, great! If you are uncomfortable or feel put upon or resentful, then maybe you need to make other choices. We often get stuck in situations because we don't make the final assessment about our condition. We complain, or we discuss, or we say, "Here I am again, and I don't know how I got here." He can claim his pattern or gain insight which leads to choice, which is often the essence of personal empowerment.

Step #1 is identifying the issue but step #2 is the empowerment moment. Do I want this situation, feeling, job, person in my life or not? Do I like it?

If I do, great. If I don't, of course the question becomes *what can I do about it?*

When I was a young mother, I met a woman in my neighborhood and we became friends. She had two small children, one of them being a baby the same age as my firstborn. She was a lovely, extremely talented woman friend. You probably won't even believe me when I tell you all the things she could do exceptionally well. She was a musician, a composer, and the cantor for her church; she made wedding gowns, cut my hair, and was a fabulous cook, a decorator, and mother of two young children. We had fun together and she helped me decorate and was very generous with her gifts.

As our children turned two, though, I began to feel badly when I left her company because she was judging my son who was more assertive than her child. I began to feel not accepted.

One time as I was sharing with my mentor that I always came away feeling badly after I had been with her, she said, "Then why do you spend time with her? She's supposed to be a friend and you get to choose those." A small light bulb went on! I was in my thirties and it still took someone from the outside to show me that I had a choice to not associate with people who I felt badly around. I remember feeling chagrined that I had put up with such a situation for as long as I had. It doesn't mean she wasn't a fine person, but for me at that time in my life she was a negative.

Therefore, one role with a teen is to be not only a listening ear to help them maneuver step #1 but also to help them question their own feelings in order to make real choices in step #2 and not just to fall into situations or accept negative outcomes that are within their control.

As my children were growing, even in elementary school, when they made friends, I always made it a point to ask them what they liked about their friends. I challenged them to articulate the qualities that caused them to choose each particular person as a friend. I wanted them to understand that, in fact, it is a choice who you hang around with, who you date, and who you marry; and it needs to go through gray matter to really be consciously a choice instead of something that just happens to you. Discussing it in this way also helped them to decide over time what qualities they were looking for in people who they chose for friends or later lovers.

When they became teenagers and began to date, I continued this line of inquiry. I made it clear that seeing someone as pretty was a good start, but it wasn't enough to sustain a relationship, so the question was, "What else do you like about her?" Our discussions almost became a shared joke in our family. So much was this a part of their growing up that when later in life I was once again in the dating world, they turned the tables on me and would ask my rationale for choosing men to date! What goes around comes around!

Empowerment is based on choice. Teenagers are now capable of making informed choices, formal operational choices based on adult-like thinking, but they need support to learn processes to structure decision-making.

CHOICES #2

To empower anyone is to help them to be aware that they have choices. Often as humans we get stuck in jobs, relationships, habits, and ways of thinking that feel like the round-and-round swirl of water going down a drain. This may feel like motion or sea sickness that leads us nowhere. Usually this feeling comes when we believe we have no choice in a matter.

If one of the messages we know teenagers need in order to develop themselves and their identity is that their choices have meaning, how can we be an asset to them in making choices?

Three techniques we can offer teens (or anyone) to enhance their ability to make good choices that lead to theory building and the formation of identity are:

1. Teach the decision-making process explicitly (earlier in book).

2. Teach them to reflect on the choices they make before and after the fact.

3. Teach them to focus on a *how/what* approach to life instead of a *why* approach.

For example: *How* do I handle this now? *What* can I do about this situation? The *why* approach often leads to self-pity and being immobilized.

Once a colleague came to me with this query: her daughter had a friend from early childhood, who she had been very close to. The families had also been friends for many years and shared in activities. Sadly, the young woman went away to college and had a severe asthma attack in the early spring of her first year and passed away. Naturally, this was a horrible blow to all who knew her.

The complication for her daughter came with the fact that in their senior year in high school, she and her friend had had a falling out and had not spoken since. In fact, the adults had continued to have a relationship. Her question to her mom, passed on to me, was that she was wondering if she should go to the funeral. Her fears were that it might be awkward; the girl's family might have negative feelings about her. They might be resentful.

My response was this: from either choice she makes, she will learn. If she goes, she will be able to face her fears, have a chance to let the family know of her feelings and possibly feel some reconciliation. If she doesn't go, she may feel peace with this, or she may regret it, and this will give her inside information to carry into future personal dilemmas.

Her mom can help by asking her, "What do you think might happen if you do go? What are your fears about going?" The most important questions to ask her, though, are, "How might you feel if you do go, and how will you feel if you don't go?" In the end she can help her reflect on her experience either way. It might be a lesson she never forgets.

When I was twenty-one, my grandma died in Chicago. She was eighty-six, and I did not go to the funeral because I didn't feel at the time that I had the money. I have always regretted my choice. I loved my grandma; she was the only grandparent I ever knew. I have many cousins and aunts and uncles who were there, and it would have been a very important family bonding time, while honoring my grandma. The consequence of that choice is that I always go to funerals of family members held in other areas, no matter the cost. I don't ever want to regret that again. My choice helped develop my theory about how to handle death in my family. I live by my theory; it's a part of how I see who I am. I believe I am family-oriented. I want to be close to my family and to show support in tough times. This one choice, although negative in the end, helped define my identity.

An educator, George Foreman says, "Experience is not the best teacher; reflection upon experience is the best teacher." By asking the questions that lead to reflection before and after a choice is made, we are facilitating identity formation. If we make all the decisions for a young person, or if we belittle their choices or ignore helping them to think things through, we are missing opportunities to support their emotional development.

Through the dialogue we are also clearly saying that you in fact do have choices and insight into how to make decisions. I believe in your choices, translated once again to support the message, *your choices have meaning. I have faith in you.*

WHAT WERE YOU THINKING?

When we offer a two-year-old a choice to wear their blue shirt or their red shirt today, we feel like a wonderfully evolved parent who understands the particular needs of a two-year-old. We tell the child enthusiastically, "You made a choice; you like the blue one today."

On the contrary when our teenager makes a choice, we yell, "What were you thinking?" Clearly, we don't have the ability to control the environment of a teen as we do with a two-year-old, but the choices of a teen are as vital to their psychological health as to the two-year-old. (I know you are probably thinking, more so.)

If you look at your own life as an adult, I'm sure you don't believe all of your choices were good ones, but hopefully you see that your choices had meaning. At our college they have a policy for students called *the right to fail.* This may sound harsh, but obvious. Students have the freedom to take responsibility for their own learning, either way. I have seen student after student begin college by failing and learning life lessons from this choice and coming back strong to pursue what they want, not what someone else believed was the correct path. Practicing making choices and then evaluating consequences is something we can support in our young person.

So, what *were* they thinking?

You remember your first kiss, the first time you stepped out of a plane and saw a country that had just been a picture in a book before, the first car you bought, the first time you stood in front of the Grand Canyon or Niagara Falls. The firsts are memorable. Not all kisses are remembered. Waterfalls, although all incredible, will never strike you as the first one did. As you progress through life, along with wisdom does come a little *been there, done that* feeling.

What the adolescent thinks comes with this newness to thinking deeply about life. It isn't thoughts based on experience but kind of a raw process that is still experimental in nature. A normal teen believes that they are invincible, so now is the time to try things, step out, or experiment. They have heard about the distant country or the waterfall, but they need to see it for themselves. They have heard you can get pregnant, become addicted to drugs, or kill someone with your car, but they don't believe it will happen to them.*

One answer to "What were you thinking?" from the teen is, "I know this may have negative consequences, but I don't think it will happen to me."

Sometimes adults mistake this process and believe they are not thinking. These are two different activities. Risky behavior can often be exciting; and if you totally believed no negative would come your way, I'm sure even many more adults would take the curves like a race-car driver.

A better learning experience they could draw from in the future may be for you to talk with your teen about real-life events.

When you hear of a teen who has committed suicide, this is a good time to say, "Why do you think someone would commit suicide? They say that most people contemplate it at some time in their life." See what your child comes up with. You may be surprised with the depth of their thought on this. It also could be a time to share an experience you have had with a family member or friend who had committed suicide or attempted it. You can say, of course, that you don't know the exact reason, but these are some of the things you wondered about related to this person's action.

This same strategy can apply to sex or drugs. Bring it up related to someone in the news or someone you know or yourself and start a dialogue. If you listen more than talk and make no judgment or know-it-all statements, then your child will be open to exploring these topics with you. Even if they don't have the whole picture yet, don't jump in to correct or teach. Validate their thoughts on the issue, even if they say something you don't agree with.

For example, a sad story in our family happened at my niece's eight-year-old birthday slumber party. Gently said, her father did not wake up that morning on the screened-in porch because of a combination of drugs and alcohol that stopped his heart. He was thirty-five years old. Gene was not setting out to kill himself that day, but his addictions did. Her father had a difficult upbringing, an alcoholic mother, no involved father, and was in a group home as an adolescent. You can imagine the trauma to everyone connected to the death. Dramatically we got called from the pulpit by the priest to come to the back of the church. Our children were eight, six, and one.

That very day we told our children what had happened. We also explained that this did not take away from his love for them or their love for him. It didn't mean he was a bad person, but it did mean he had made some very destructive choices. Gene's death was a life lesson learned early by my children on the dangers of drugs and alcohol. Certainly, we wish it had never happened; we wish he had not been in such internal pain that he had to hide it in chemicals, but we did use it as an example to our children over the years.

If you don't know why something happened, discuss it with your children. Why do you think someone would need to take drugs, or drink to the point of being addicted? Not that you are telling them what to think, but you are exploring together the vagaries of the human mind and heart.

* Invincibility Theory: Alberts, Elkind, and Ginsburg, 2007

PARENTING IS HUMBLING

Parenting by its very nature is humbling. We want to do our best job ever in being a parent. But no matter how spectacular we are, what we have as a product in the end is a human being, a beautiful, magnificent, flawed human being.

The criteria for success are also varied. Are you only to be judged when it's over, when they are a grown productive member of society? Or are you constantly being judged as your two-year-old throws a tortilla chip in the crowded restaurant and hits a woman who is not amused? When your teenager is suspended for fighting? When the middle school calls because your child has written his name on a desk? When the police call you from the station? How do we know if we're doing a good job?

So, my advice is to start out humbled with your teenager. You don't have to be the source of all knowledge anymore. You don't have to have answers to every question. You don't have to protect yourself and cover your past sins and confusions. It's time for you to be your real self if you've been hiding behind some parent role up until now.

Adolescents are ready for real life. They need our processes, our foibles, our missteps as framework for a life.

Einstein said, "The only real question is.... is the universe safe?" I believe the fundamental question for parents and for teenagers is, "Is it normal? Am I normal?" I'm not exactly sure why we so want to be told we are normal, while fighting diligently to be unique, but it is one of those both/and realities.

When we share our stories, we are saying to our child that we are not perfect either, that we struggled and stumbled and we're still standing. This is hope; the very successful Alcoholics Anonymous group is based on this very hope. If I can get a footing, I can build a life from there. Right now, says the teen, I'm not sure of my footing (*Who Am I?*), but if I hear others were not always so sure, it is a relief to me that allows me to take a deep breath and focus on forward movement. I once heard it said by a wise one, "I've been to the bottom and it's solid." The solid ground for the teen is not the perfection of others but the stories that show we are all in the mud together. It's the human condition, the people of the ground, the earth. The knowledge that I am not alone in my inside, I am not the only one, is a saving understanding for the teen.

How does one proceed to share themselves as a real person now that they have a teen?

Often by reflecting their feelings and thoughts back to them, we can achieve a trust and closeness based on what they talk about or bring to us. The humble parent can also initiate ideas about their life, current or past.

Unfortunately, when my daughter was thirteen her father and I divorced; our sons were eighteen and twenty-one. My daughter-in-law has told me that my son probably felt the closest to me when I truly told him my perspective on the reasons for the divorce. They weren't from a place of blaming myself or their dad, but my feelings about what had happened. It did not paint me in such a beautiful light but was very raw and real, since I was the one who initiated the separation and he is a good guy. When someone is at their most real and vulnerable, we have the most connection because at any age this is a state we can relate to.

Many times, parents who were the most raucous teens are the hardest on their own children, or women who were sexually molested or raped over-protect their daughters but never tell them why. Often, then, this teen just feels as if her parent doesn't trust her. The opportunity is missed to show trust and connection. I'm a person who has had struggles and this is how they have affected me, and this is what I have learned from it. Then you have two winners, and your own telling of your own story can help heal it for you also.

DON'T SAY, "HELL, NO!"

When my daughter was in high school, she was not all that thrilled with school by her junior year. She had friends but was thinking about quitting high school and getting a GED. Since her father and I have given our whole working life to education, needless to say, this idea did not thrill me. One of the things that concerned me was what would she do with all that time on her hands.

My biggest concern I shared with her. I listened empathetically and acknowledged that junior year could be one of the toughest because it felt long and tedious. I mentioned that senior year sometimes was an improvement because there were a lot of activities just for seniors and you had the senior status thing going on.

I told her that I believed there was a bias by the culture and possibly even colleges that a GED was not as good as, did not have as much status as, a high school diploma. I suggested that I could be wrong, though, and encouraged her to ask other people to see if they felt the bias I described. She came to me a few weeks later and shared that other people she had talked to believed, as I did. Usually one thing we don't want as teenagers is any type of avoidable low status being projected our way. She changed her mind and decided to stick it out in high school.

Her choices have meaning. They are motivated by needs she has, but since she is able to think like an adult, she can use input from others if she seeks it out on her own and believes that she has a choice to make about her life. Teenagers are poised to create their own story. When we have no faith in their ability to write it for themselves, we force them into using all their energy defending their right to make choices or hiding from us. When we provide honest, respectful feedback to their ideas and encourage them to seek other ideas as well, we support what they are doing anyway, and what they need to do to develop theories about life and how to be in the world.

The metaphor I use for all parenting is the baby who is learning to walk. When they take their first steps, we crouch down and encourage them, "Come on; walk to Mommy," knowing full well they will fall.

We don't say, "Sit down, don't walk; you are going to fall." We know they need to fall to learn to control their movements and balance, and yet we encourage them! Throughout each stage of parenting, one needs to practice this type of encouragement. *I'm here with a smile and open arms, but you are going to fall, and I believe you can handle it.* I will help my children by learning the right type of encouragement for each stage.

By listening with empathy, giving honest, respectful feedback, and encouraging them to look for other sources besides you in making decisions, we help empower them and free them to make their own mistakes while learning to walk, to find their own unique balance.

Recently, visiting an elementary school I saw this on a bulletin board in a hallway: "Mistakes help your brain grow."

I once heard a story on the radio of an adult recounting a tale of his youth. In those days one could buy cigarettes from a vending machine. He was about fourteen and the legal age to buy them was eighteen. An owner of the local store saw him trying to buy the cigarettes and told him he didn't want him to because they would harm him, and it wasn't legal anyway. He remembered this man many years later because he was shocked and pleased that someone cared enough to stop him from a negative behavior. I know the man never thanked the store owner or in any way let him know how much his care had meant at such a vulnerable time in his life. The stranger showed care and concern. Note: he did not tell him he couldn't buy them or use a forceful attitude. In one way it's a sad story because it was such a small thing. Did the young man have so little concern for his well-being communicated by others? One wonders how much our teens actually hear of our care as opposed to our expectations, demands, and worries.

BALANCE

A well-known infant-toddler expert, Magda Gerber* once said that balance is a life-long pursuit. She was speaking of physical balance. Watching a baby practice through movement and beginning walking—this is clear to see. Watching an older person maneuver through the world adds another level of clarity to her point. But in the world of parenting, we need to establish balance of high-wire proportions. How much do we monitor our teenagers? What is enough? Too much? Too little? It is clear there can be too much or too little. Balance is the ticket to support that is life-giving and not stifling. Like offering a toddler just one finger when they reach out as they begin to fall off a balance beam, we want to offer the least amount of help that will allow the teen to make their own choices, claim their own life, and get credit for the way their life is going.

From the time you are a toddler you need to do things in the world *all by yourself* to gain confidence and resilience. Rescuing, taking over, should be things of the past with our teens.

As a young college freshman about 400 miles from home, my son was coming home for Christmas vacation. He had his first big romance at that time at school. We made him come home on the greyhound bus trying to teach him the value of money and that not everyone was as lucky as he, in regards, to opportunities in life. It was an experience he still talks about to this day. Because his school is five miles away from the bus station, he had taken a taxi for $10 to the bus depot. He was left with $50 in his pocket as he headed home. While he was home, he wanted to buy his girlfriend a Christmas present and he saw a $50 stuffed bear that he thought she would like. He mentioned this to his father and me, and all we said was, "Make sure you have enough money left to get home from the bus station to the college." He was our first-born and we were serious, as only first-time parents of each stage can be, about teaching him the value of money. Of course, he went out and bought the bear; and then as you can deduce, he now had no money left. His bus was going to arrive in the college town at midnight and none of his college friends had cars. My husband and I talked about what we should do and decided we shouldn't rescue him by giving him money. We agreed after a long discussion that we were being good and responsible parents teaching him the important lessons to protect him for the future. His father drove him to the bus station on the appointed day. Our son seemed fairly unconcerned. Naturally, I was nervous about the arrival on the other end, but we had agreed on what was best for our son. We both felt badly, and I worried until I heard he had made it back safely to campus. I felt righteously satisfied, though, that we were excellent parents.

It was years later that my husband admitted to me that he had in fact given him the $10 at the bus station. He caved into his fear, but I must admit, I understood. Oh well, the value of money would be learned another day.

Sure enough, the next year his friends and he got an apartment. He had a job at the school and was paying for things besides rent and school. He called me one day and in a horrified voice said, "Mom, do you know how much deodorant costs?" "Yes, son, I actually do." He said, "I had to work a half hour just to pay for that deodorant!" Bingo, the value of money and work was beginning to take up space in his brain!

*Magda Gerber a well-known writer and teacher in the area of Child Development, co-founded Resources for Infant-Educators, an educational philosophy that helps parents and teachers to really see their children.

MY FIRST CAR

When I was a teenager, I wanted a car. I remember clearly that my dad said he would give me $500 for the down payment and I could make the payments. I loved my 1966 used VW bug and learned to drive a stick shift lurching around town for a few days in that car. I had a job and was going to school. I remember feeling so proud of myself in making the payments—that it was my car. I assume my dad could have made the payments for me, but it is such a strong memory. I don't remember most of the things they bought for me or paid for, but I do remember the pride I had in myself that I was taking care of my own life.

We give our children a gift by giving them opportunities to feel pride in their own accomplishments rather than just giving them everything on a platter. Real-life lessons speak louder than words and just *doing for them* what they can do for themselves.

GREEN HAIR

When my daughter was in eighth grade, she and a couple of her friends were at the house. It was spring. One of her talkative friends pipes up, "Natalie wants to have green hair." I could see that my daughter was a little uncomfortable with this revelation. I want you to know this is a while ago and green hair was just beginning to be a thing, and inside I must admit, I was not thrilled with the idea of her having green hair. Let's just put it this way: no child at my church or in our circle of friends had green hair at the time.

In a moment of what quite possibly was an inspiration from above, though, what I said was, "Oh, green hair," in an interested but non-judgmental voice. Her friend then said that the junior high would not allow green hair. I responded with another inspired phrase, "Well, maybe you can have it in the summer."

When her friends left that day, I wanted to explore this issue, so I just said, "So you want green hair?" a perfect reflective listening response. It had the desired effect. She said, "I just want to be noticed." Now we were really communicating! By remaining open, non-judging, interested, I had allowed her to reveal more of her real self. I was gaining access to her thoughts and feelings, exactly the outcome the parent of a teenager should want, a building of trust and communication. In this way I have a chance of being a resource for her in her life, and I also build a true, more adult relationship with my child. This is the only chance that she can *tell me anything*, a phrase parents use with their children but often don't know how to bring about.

Now I could truly understand her. I said, "I like to be noticed too, and especially at your age, I did." The outcome of this encounter was that she never had green hair, not because I wouldn't let her, not because I decided I didn't like it, but she came to this decision. My guess is that just being really and truly heard, having someone acknowledge her needs and who she was, allowed her to make her own decision. She didn't need to take a reactionary position and rebel against my will, my *no*. She was free to have her own choices. She was supported, and we were able to share some of the same human feelings. I essentially had the chance to tell her that she was normal! If I had said *no* and gone off on all my reasons, at that point I would have missed an opportunity for connection, a chance to let her know that her choices have meaning, and that she has power to make choices. When a teenager is pushed into a corner, they will push back; they need to in order to say, "I'm not you, Mom, Dad. I have to build my own theories." Their job is to build their identity, remember, and we can get in the way or we can act as a supportive backdrop, a resource for their ultimate decision. It all depends on those few minutes of choice we have when confronted with a teenage statement or dilemma.

Take time. Reflect back what you hear them say. Wait. Listen.

WORLD OF YES

A few years ago, I often frequented a yogurt shop on my way to work. The young man who worked there and I made some connection. For some unexplained reason we had some deep conversations about life, but in the most simple format. He would often say things I would think about later. Once Raphael provided a metaphor for a way of experiencing childhood that I believe should be a philosophical underpinning of childhood and really of all life. He had grown up in Mexico on some ranch land. He said that he and his cousins had "complete freedom to explore the world around them but they knew their boundaries." Someone parented him and his cousins well. They felt freedom as children but knew what would not be acceptable.

For me this is the *world of yes* we should all inhabit. The world should be a world of *yes*, with a few, clear, absolute *no's*. Children should not be restricted constantly. The freedom to be, explore, and discover need to be a part of a healthy childhood, even if we need to create this space for the child.

Everyone does not have the idyllic world of a ranch or for that matter a safe neighborhood to explore, but I am talking even more of a psychological state that allows the child to dream, create, inquire, move, and believe, in the *yes*. This may in fact be the freedom we are always seeking.

At the park recently, I observed a couple of young women and several children. The young women continually told the children what to do even though they were not doing anything wrong. "Come over here; get away from the water fountain; don't do that." Nothing the children were doing was bothersome to any other person or destructive, or dangerous, (all legitimate activities) yet they were constantly being told, "'The world is a *no world*." When you are constantly being directed, what is the result? Children become discouraged, rebellious, and doubt themselves.

In my class of college students, I do an exercise. I have them stand up and then give them directions, in rapid succession. For example,

"Don't sit down, don't smile, don't stand up, don't look at me, look at me, stand up, etc." At the end the students tell me that they didn't know what to do. They felt badly about themselves and were anxious. Being directed verbally constantly produces anxiety, which later can lead to rebellion and feelings of unworthiness. Children explore all new things from the moment they can. This is their natural state to learn about the world. Of course, the adults on the planet need to teach children right from wrong, but there really shouldn't be, and in fact are not, as many wrongs as there are rights for most people most of the time.

In a market the other day I heard this same scenario repeated with about a five-year-old boy but even in a harsher manner. The child was not doing anything wrong but was told, "Get over here. I'm going to hit you," etc. when in fact he was just standing by the cart and walking down the aisle of the market. How can a child flourish in such a negative system?

A world of *yes* is the world we inhabit. I can do anything I want except for the things I can't do: things that hurt others, damage property, or endanger someone or myself. Most of my day I have many choices and freedoms. A child who dwells in the land of *yes* can create a healthy world. They can find their limits, and they will have the freedom to add something unique to the world. They will know their boundaries and live within them because their freedom is respected; their personhood and preferences are respected.

The world of *yes* particularly needs to be the experience of teenagers. As long as they are doing the basics to take care of their life, they should have freedom to choose. If they step out of the boundaries we have set as their parents, through dialogue and the setting of standards throughout their life so far, then they need to be pulled back inside those boundaries and experience a consequence to be reminded or educated about the limits set for their benefit. *I want you to live the life you love, child of mine. I want you to bloom into who you are. I want you to create a life for yourself of happiness and creativity. Just stay within these wide boundaries for your good and the good of others.* This is what I want them to know. It's a world of *yes*. It truly can be.

WORLD OF YES, PART 2

An environment of *yes* has as its cornerstone an attitude of freedom for the child/teenager to be who they are, to be fully the person they want or need to be. When a teenager expresses a desire to do something, our first thoughts should not be, *no, absolutely not!* Even if those are our first thoughts, we can wait to express our concerns. They shouldn't be our first words. The *no* reaction comes from fear. We immediately see, as adults, all the scary/dangerous/or problematic outcomes for our child, who we desire to protect at all costs. But this hasty *no* is not good parenting. Our first reaction will be most productive if we communicate to the adolescent that we actually *want* them to do what they desire. I believe we feel as if we are giving up power, but if we want power, we can always have it. What we need to cultivate with our teenager is *empowerment* for their benefit, not power for our comfort.

When my daughter was a freshman in high school, she asked if she could go to midnight bowling at an alley in a town about twelve miles from our home. I'd been to the bowling alley and it was a fine place. I asked who was going and what they were planning. Her response was that her group of four good friends were going, and a mother was going to drop them off and pick them up.

They would bowl while there was at the time music and a light show experience going on at midnight bowling. All parts I could understand to be attractive to young teenage girls. My first thought was, *a bowling alley at midnight, young girls with no adult supervision, guys drinking beer, etc.* I was uncomfortable with my picture of the scene, for my daughter. But instead of saying *no*, I asked her for more details, told her honestly of my picture of guys drinking beer and my worries of her safety in that environment. Her response was that "Everyone else is going". Still with an open mind but my own discomforts, I said I would call Kelly's Mom who was to drive them and talk with her about it. I followed through with this and found she was comfortable having the girls go and not being with them to supervise. I told her of my concerns and that I wasn't sure what I would decide. I talked to my daughter about what the mom and I had talked about; but in my mind and insides, I still felt uncomfortable. I reiterated my image of young girls on their own, late at night with older guys around drinking. I just wasn't comfortable. I told her all of this. I empathized that I knew it sounded fun and maybe when she was a senior in high school it would be more reasonable to me. I told her I knew it would be difficult to be the only one who couldn't go. If she could get a parent to go and stay, I could let her go. We had quite a dialogue over a couple of days, but it all centered around me honestly sharing my fears and feelings and listening openly to her point of view. But in the end, I still said *no* and she in fact did not go and all her friends did. She said, "Oh, Mom" in a semi-exasperated voice and that was the end of it. I asked her after the first day back at school if she had felt badly that she missed out and she told me it was no big deal.

I wanted to say *yes*. I tried to say *yes*, but I was her parent and I need to, in the end, set standards that I am comfortable with. I didn't judge others' standards; I just knew that my job was to live by mine with my children, while they were still not adults. She knew that I respectfully listened to her point of view, that I explored possibilities that I was comfortable with that would lead to a *yes*, but these didn't happen. It's a world of *yes* and the *no* is a respectful *no*.

There were times I was the parent who let my children do activities other parents were not comfortable with and that was OK too.

And another thing… When you feel the urge to say *no* to a teenage scheme, take a breath and wait and listen. Say something noncommittal like, "Tell me more about that." Act interested and positive. You will have time to explore your own ideas and feelings later. Definitely don't jump to *no*, or *yes* for that matter, too quickly.

Once they have explained what they want to do—drive to Tijuana this weekend, go on a camping trip with seventeen of their best friends, etc.—then you have the chance to let them know your boundaries. For example, "That sounds fun, and as long as you have an adult going for supervision, I think it would be OK." In other words, set your boundary and let them figure out how to meet your standards. Sometimes the plans fall through anyway, and if not, if you have truly thought through what you would be comfortable with, then you can be fine with your *yes*.

BAD BEHAVIOR? SAYS WHO?

When a toddler bites another toddler in a day care, some people flip out and overreact and make the issue more difficult. It is within the normal range of development for a toddler to bite. It is a behavior motivated by a need of the toddler and it is not OK. We need to protect the other children and find out why the child is biting. Not so difficult. If we focus only on the actual biting as a bad behavior, we have missed the opportunity for this child to grow into a fully integrated respected person.

It is the same for teens. If we only focus on the *bad* behavior, (getting drunk, doing drugs, running away, ditching school, lying, etc.) and don't read the need, we've missed a great chance for valuable learning about a hugely important skill… how to be a person! One of my friends when he was in his fifties used to say, "I think I'm still grounded." In other words, his parents had attacked the bad behavior with grounding him so many times that it all had become meaningless. Similar to spanking a child, often the child remembers the punishment but not the lesson—pretty much useless.

If you want to help your teenager, or child, make sure you differentiate behavior. Is getting a tattoo vine around your belly button or shoulder a bad behavior? Is listening to music I don't like a bad behavior? Is making your hair into rainbow stripes or wearing your clothes too tight or too loose a bad behavior?

Make sure you separate things you don't like from character issues that will harm your child or others. Intervene on the character issues without fail, no matter the age of the child. Behaviors you don't like but aren't inherently wrong can be items of opportunity to communicate, to understand, and to accept their choices. Remember, you can always honestly talk about your concerns or feelings about these choices, but usually it works against your relationship with them if you take everything to the mat. When you completely get stuck on the behavior and not the need behind it, you can cause resentment on the part of your child. Often people scream their needs and they don't even know they have their mouth open. Most of the time the teen doesn't even realize the need they are acting out; in other words, the discomfort of the need comes out in another way. All people do this in some form or for some period of time. We yell and scream, throw something, don't speak; use food, alcohol, drugs, sex, or overwork to deal with feelings or needs that we have, but can't manage to accept or fulfill.

The basic needs as Abraham Maslow, an American psychologist, tells us in his classic description of our "hierarchy of needs" are that we first need to have our physical needs met, i.e., our needs for food, water, shelter, etc. The psychological needs become a little trickier and less obvious. Stanley Coopersmith, an articulate psychologist, described these needs in a succinct and helpful way. Often when I am acting in ways that don't make initial sense to me, such as when I am angry, hurt, or sad and don't really understand why, I look at these four needs and see if one is out of whack. Often, I can identify the source of my acting out. Next time you have a bad day, see if any of these needs have not been met that day. The four needs he describes are: significance, competence, power, and virtue.

If you were criticized at work, you may deep down feel incompetent. You might act this out as anger at the person who criticized you, but if you can recognize that you felt incompetent after the criticism, then you have a choice to do something about it instead of acting grumpy and yelling at people. The old stereotypical family joke was: Dad has a bad day at work, he yells at his wife, the wife yells at the kids, and the kids kick the dog. Now you can see if there is something you can change from the criticism. If it was not correct in your judgment, you may decide to discuss it in some way with the person. You might make a list of all the areas in your life, or all the things you did that day, that were competent. You might make a delicious dinner because you are an excellent cook, to restore your faith in your own competence. You might tell someone about your feelings, and their listening will help you claim the areas in which you know you are competent.

I don't believe that spanking is a good way to teach lessons to children, but I did spank my children a few times. Looking at it now,

I am able to see it was always when I felt incompetent. I didn't know what to do in relation to what they did that brought out my feelings of inadequacy, so I spanked them out of my anger at being made to feel incompetent. It wasn't about trying to teach them a lesson but my feelings that were somewhat out of control.

Remember the story of my daughter and the green hair. She was able to say her need, "I want to be noticed" (significance). Listening with no judgment helped her to be able to articulate her need. In that case her need for attention was made clear to her. I gave her attention and then she had more control over how she could get attention because she had identified her need. *Do I want or need green hair? Is that going to do it? Are there other ways I can get this need met? Do I just have to be heard and that alone meets the need?*

I know from personal experience that your first child becoming a teen can be frightening because when they do make a bad choice and behave in a way that is wrong or shocking to you, it is scary. You wonder, *are they going to grow up to be an ax murderer? Are they going to be a liar?* Your first time around, you as a parent don't have perspective. Trust me here. Put in your time and learn the ways to parent a teen, and they will grow up to be productive citizens. I remind you, would you want to be judged about who you are now by some of your teenage behavior? I doubt it.

SURPRISE!

Being the parent of a teenager as opposed to a child, is similar to the difference between wanting a child and actually being pregnant with one. The no going-back feeling is very different than just wishing. With teenagers, new issues come up fast and decisions need to be made. I remember wondering when my son would have his first girlfriend, and then one day he wants to know if he can go to a girl's house or meet her at the movies. What do you do today, right now?

It went from speculation to decision-making in one day, and I didn't know when or where or exactly how it would play out. What do you do with your twelve or thirteen-year-old who wants to do these things? You haven't had to deal with this before. You are new at this, but you can't wait too long to make a stab at it.

Your child arrives home drunk and this is your first experience with this. You have to do something, but you haven't thought of what because one day they were a kid and now this. Sex, drugs, rock and roll, decisions to be made, different in timing for every teen. Different teens, different issues, different timing. Some situations you will never face; others will feel too soon, and you will ask yourself, "Is this normal?"

Breathe, breathe, breathe! Step one.

The surprise of new developments is part of the challenge of parenting a teen. You can't say, "I'm having a bad week at work. Can we deal with this in a couple of weeks?"

First thought, breathe; second, listen; third, communicate.

In other words, you do have an hour or a day, take it. Breathe; then listen to your child. Ask them: "What do you want to do? What do you think some of my concerns will be?" (Or are, if it's already happened.) Then tell them you want to think about it overnight, or for an hour, if in fact you are confused. If there are two parents, talk to each other. You can even tell them that you have never been through this before as a parent so will need some time to think about it. "I want you to have what you want, but I also want to keep you from getting hurt or doing something that can harm you."

Then, tell your child your honest concerns. Remember, "I feel concerned because...."

Don't forget to also acknowledge that what they want, of course, is normal and natural. "It's exciting to like a girl," or, "I know sometimes young people experiment with alcohol." You can tell a pertinent mishap from your own youth here if it applies. You want them to know that you appreciate their feelings. You don't want them to misunderstand and perceive that you think that rules or teaching them a lesson is more important than they are. When we go into our teaching mode before listening, we often don't ever get to an understanding of another person's point of view. That other person is not a stranger on the street but the person we are most motivated to know.

V

Message #3— I Won't Give Up on You

NO WORDS – I WON'T GIVE UP ON YOU

The world of adolescence is decidedly more complex than the childhood years. Mainly, as you have seen, this is a developmental phenomenon. Keep in mind that *time does heal all things*, and that much of the angst of the teen years comes from the changes hitting the wall of lack of experience.

A young woman I know was being sexually molested by her grandfather when she was a young teen. Another person I know lost her mother when she was thirteen. A student of mine was molested by a family friend and never told anyone until he told me, when I was his professor in college. Several folks I know well, lived with alcoholic parents during their teen years. Their friends didn't know about these things, or in the case of death, didn't know what to do about it. These people had good friends during these years. They all said their friends were there for them, but still they did not know about these life-shaping events that were going on in the lives of their best friends. When I first heard of these types of situations and the dynamics with friends, it challenged me. How could this be that young teens don't share these types of events, even with those closest to them? These were not withdrawn or loner kids.

I have come to believe that it is not that the teen is hiding but that the young person doesn't have the words. Part of the issue is a sense of common *victim shame*, that somehow it is their fault that these bad things happen to them. But a more compelling factor is the inability to find the language to express what is going on. Remember, they are new to this level of thought: an abstract, hypothetical thought that can explain issues from many different angles and articulate positions and hypothesis of how and why things come to be.

It is imperative then that we learn to observe and confront young people when behavior of any kind changes or when we have that intuition that something is wrong. Most of these people, now as adults, told me of the particular dynamics of their family. They were afraid to tell their parents because someone else in the family was involved, and they were frightened of anger or judgment. But with their friends, it is the inability to understand the experience clearly enough to talk about it.

We know as adults it is very difficult to go through things without the support of family and/or friends. It is the same for teens. Adults often don't know what is actually wrong, but they feel uneasiness coming from the child. Follow these intuitions and you will discover the real issue.

By using our feelings, our relationship with the child, we can address what might be happening. So many times, I have told a friend of mine what was going on in my life in relation to someone I care about. I often will end with, "I don't know how to bring this up." She will say, "Just say it like you said it to me." She's right! Honesty truly is the best policy.

When we are scared for our child, we need to say it. "I know something is not right with you. I'm not sure what you are struggling with or trying to hide, but I know there is something." Then wait, silently. Maybe just this will cause the child to open-up, but maybe not.

Don't allow, "Nothing's wrong."

I might say, "I love you too much to let that pass as an answer. Just like you can tell when things aren't right with me, I can tell something is going on. Sometimes things just seem not right inside of us, but usually this comes from something that happened to us and then we are stuck in our head about it."

Two other strategies might be helpful here: One is to tell some experiences young people have struggled with. For example, you may say, "I know people who have been molested, or are taking drugs, or feel worthless, or are being bullied, or are struggling with their own sexuality. At your age some of these things are common. Sometimes people judge themselves in these areas, or they think no one else has been through these things or would understand. I don't know a single person who didn't do things as a teen they would rather not have anyone know, or they would like to redo." Then wait, silently. Listen to their body language and their words.

If they walk away, you let them but let them know, "If you are not ready to talk about this now, that's fine, but I'm not letting it go. I love you too much."

The second strategy is to set some limits or guidelines. You need to do this with confidence. The message, remember, is, "I won't give up on you." For example, "I know you want to blow me off, but I love you too much to watch you not feel well. So, you are going to have to do some things until I see that you feel better. When people are depressed or uncomfortable, there are proactive things they can do. You need to eat right and make sure you are getting your nutrients. Believe it or not, you can make yourself depressed by not eating right. You need to exercise at least three times a week, and you need to find a place you can volunteer once a week, because helping someone else helps us to gain perspective. So, until you feel better or are willing to talk, you will have to do these things. You think about where you want to volunteer and what exercise you will do, and we'll talk again tomorrow."

"I also want you to talk to someone about what is going on in your head. It can be me, a friend, a psychologist... someone. When you get stuck in your own head, it can be like quicksand. You let me know tomorrow who you decide to talk with also."

In this you require some things of the teen. Often it is a relief to the young person to have a focus. They might complain, but they are still your child and you can require them to fulfill good solid, healthy practices that any psychologist will tell you are the place to start to grab hold of your own life. These are adult ideas; these are real strategies that can be applied over and over throughout their lives to deal with the peaks and valleys ahead.

Families who have teens with obvious substance abuse have taken them to rehab. They have required it. This is legitimate. The message is, "I will not let you throw your life away. I love you too much. I will do everything I can to make sure that doesn't happen."

Try to leave some element of choice if you can. Of course, this depends on the extent of the addiction. Possibly they can have a choice to go to AA or NA meetings and talk to a psychologist who deals with this or a treatment center. As I said, this depends on the extent of the danger the child is in.

Does this mean your child will magically change? Does this mean they will respond to rehab? They still are a person with choices, but there is no more powerful force on the planet than a relationship of love. *I won't give up on you* can be the most powerful life-changing words you have ever spoken to your child.

It seems that even with the people we love most, we often just live comfortably beside them sharing life and the everydayness of things. This is all good. It is a need and pleasure as a person to have family and loves that we choose to take on in life. The flip side is that we don't always talk at the deep level about what we need, who we are, how we feel, even about each other. Someone I love will some-times say, "You know I love you." It's true, I do. But words are impor-tant. The conventional saying is, "Actions speak louder than words." But never did this negate the incredible power of words, especially if our words are a true reflection of our current feelings. These are the words you remember all your life. I have been working with people for over thirty-five years, and I could fill more than an encyclopedia with memories that people have shared about words that were said that have stayed with them throughout their lives and shaped them. Good, bad, and indifferent, words do matter.

HOPE—YOU ARE RIGHT WHERE YOU ARE SUPPOSED TO BE

At the worst time of my life, my twenty-seven-year marriage was falling apart. Everything I knew about myself was thrown up in the air, and I wasn't sure when the pieces fell if they would ever be put back together. In this scattered Humpty Dumpty state, a friend I had since, ironically enough, my fifteenth year, said to me, "You're right where you are supposed to be."

The most powerful, freeing words I had ever heard in my life, truly, were these words. In the middle of my worst self, my worst performance as a human being, he said it was nothing to fight against. What he gave me was hope.

Most people in my life didn't know that I thought of dying, that I was scared, that it took all my attention just to focus on my daily life. From the outside, I looked fairly fine. I got a new job as a professor and functioned well at it. I was raising my teenage daughter and tried to help her through the earthquake. Most people did not know, just like most teenagers, the inside may be hidden from view, not because they are consciously hiding but they don't have the words.

I didn't have the words because I didn't see a life on the other side. I couldn't picture this new life. I couldn't process with friends something I had no idea about.

The third message our young person needs to feel from us is, "You are right where you are supposed to be." When you are at your worst, you feel badly about yourself and feel isolated and confused. You think that no one has felt like this; you don't see a light at the end of your tunnel, and you need someone to hold the hope for you. Our job, if we want to help the teenager to keep going successfully, is to carry the hope for them.

They need us to reflect, "Ah, what I see in you." They can't see what they will be. They haven't had experience as adult thinkers swimming through difficult waters. They don't know they will or can make it. That awareness takes experience of having made it through challenging times.

The world is telling them that they are messed up and that their choices are ridiculous, and their bodies are beyond their control. Demands are many and they get very little positive feedback from the outside and virtually none from the inside. Even the most together, successful teenager on the outside needs this message from us. We need to reflect the future and present that we see:

- "You are so talented at singing. This will be used in your life for something really special. I just know"

- "You are so kindhearted, the way you treat your grandma shows me what a loving person you are and will continue to be."

- "You have so many friends. You obviously know how to be a good friend, and this will carry over into your whole life as such an asset, even in your work life."

- "The way you quietly think things through before you speak, I think, is a sign of a very intelligent mind. People in the world appreciate that quality."

- "You clearly have a talent for judo and you are so determined; both those things will really lead to so much discipline and success in your life."

Do you see? We need to expressly *hold the hope* and explicitly point out, "'What I see in you…" Every teenager needs this, even if they seem fine on the outside. We need to be looking for these opportunities to show a hope for them that is, of course, there. We are doing this to inoculate them against the pitfalls of their *normal* developmental stage.

At some time in your young life someone probably said, "You have your whole life ahead of you." Sometimes it was said to indicate that you should be grateful for this fact. Sometimes it was said to make you feel that what you are feeling right now is trivial and not as important as adult problems.

These are not the messages teenagers need. They need to hear messages such as these, the more specific you can be, the better:

- "Yes, it is hard to be a teenager, but I see a future of many experiences that are ahead for you that are life-giving and beautiful."

- "Not just because you are young but what I uniquely see in you. You have so much to give to the world. I know your interest and ability working with animals will be a talent you can use."

- "You are so tuned into people's feelings; you are observant. That is a skill that will serve you well."

- "Your art is so appealing; it gives me a serene feeling." The more specific you can be, the better.

When someone tells you, "You look nice," that feels good, but they can be telling that just as a pleasantry which many people do almost as a greeting to friends. If someone says, "That blue color brings out the beautiful glow of your face," this is much more valuable. One, you know the person took time to notice and say it and that it was specific and therefore true. Plus, you have information about what color looks good on you! The specifics help teens to have information about who they are.

When I was young, a teacher told me privately after I had given a speech that I was nervous about, that I had a real presence. He said I could command the audience and I should use my height to advantage and exhibit confidence. He told me something very specific I did not know, and I've never forgotten it. I have been a teacher in my adult life, and this ability I had was first pointed out by that teacher. I believed him because he took the time to notice, be specific, and to tell me essentially, "What I see in you..." I was nervous and new, but he held a hope for me.

Two tensions that we hold as human beings are that we want to be *normal,* and we want to be *unique.* It's a human dilemma. As you age into adulthood, you generally begin to believe both of these realities and we call this integration. When you are a teenager, you don't know yet whether you are *normal* and what type of *unique* you are. Your feelings of *nobody feels like I do* can actually be isolating at this stage of development. The two realities need to be in balance to be a fully functioning adult. (This is not to say they don't get out of whack as an adult, but we have experience about how to bring them back into balance.)

Teenagers need us to give them the message, "I won't give up on you."

To their problems, emotional outbursts, confusion, depression, success, you can say, "I won't give up on you. Go ahead and give up on yourself, but I'll be here holding the hope for you because I see so much in you that you can't see from so close up."

Once I knew a family with seven children; the father was a minister in the community. The oldest son had always pushed the boundaries as he was growing. All the other children seemingly went with the flow of the family. Evan fought everything and got in trouble out in the world as he became an adolescent. The mother and father were at their wits end, and they felt they had tried everything—punishments and consequences and talking until they were hoarse.

One day the mother told me she had this insight. Of course, being a fifteen-year-old, he liked having money of his own, so she decided to use this to try to break through to him. Every time he would talk back or buck the system of the family, she would go and put a dollar on his bed after he had gone. She didn't say anything; she stopped nagging him and just left money when he did something wrong or negative. A few days into this system, he came to her crying with shame, saying he didn't deserve to be treated with love because of how he had been acting.

Lesson learned: he knew he was screwing up, but he felt so negative about himself, so undeserving, that he was lashing out. When his mom began to say through the money, "I love you just as you are today, even in your *bad* behavior," he had a breakthrough. She held the hope for him. I won't give up on you kid, no matter what. In the face of love and hope of this kind we have no defenses.

I heard a young woman talk about her teenage ditching-school forays. Her mother was a working, single mother. The mom took her vacation days and went with her daughter to school for about a week, to make sure she was there. Of course, you can imagine the girl hated this and was embarrassed at the time. But telling this story as a young adult, she was so appreciative of her mother and knew this was an, "I won't give up on you" message. *You are too important to me for me to let you ruin your life. I will do everything in my power to make sure you succeed.* As we say, she put her time where her mouth was!

When we hold the hope, it must be genuine, not placating, and not condescending. Remember they KNOW! A difficult situation arises when your daughter comes home and says, "I hate school, and I'm not going back!" Your gut reaction may be to give a treatise on the value of an education. Another option is to say she is lucky that she can go to school and doesn't have to work. We can also make our child feel ungrateful for all that they have that other people in the world would love to have.

None of these are supportive, helpful, or really correct for a teenager. Our best bet is to reflect their feeling back to them. "You had a bad day." Your child then is much more likely to give you more information. If not at first, just stick with your reflecting their words or feelings back to them. "School sucks. You don't want to go back." Say it with an empathetic heart and voice. After a few times of this, I can almost guarantee you will get another response. If you only say that, resist the urge to ask a question or say any other words, only reflect their feeling in statements, then your child may say, "Math was hard and Juan said I had chicken legs." Now what? More of the same; reflect and nothing else. "That hurts when someone says something mean about your body, and math IS hard."

Even though you may want to, don't say, "You don't have chicken legs! You are beautiful!" No matter if it is true or seems helpful, you will stop getting to the real story. Your child might even say, "You don't understand." The communication and understanding will stop. Besides, it doesn't matter now that you think she is beautiful; she wants Juan to think she's pretty.

When you verbally empathize using the same words or feelings they are expressing, your child will tell you more. Then you will be able to hear them, and to be heard without judgment is healing.

It even gets harder. If your child says, "I hate my big nose!" You can't say, "You don't have a big nose." You need to be honest or it is useless. You say," You don't like your nose. There are parts of me I don't like too. It feels bad to not like parts of yourself." Let her feel sad; don't talk her out of it. Later after she has time to express herself, you can point out the beautiful parts she does have, that are true and lovely. "You have beautiful hair; your smile is contagious."

An important caveat for parents is that we need to give these messages with no expectation of seeing a reward or change in outward behavior now. Most of our work with teenagers is money in the bank; the interest is compounded daily, but it doesn't look like much for a long time. You will get the pay-off later, but the effort you put in now is just a pure gift for the time being.

THE ART OF THE QUESTION

I overheard two mothers of teens in a restaurant the other day. They were both discussing how their children would respond to the question, "How was school?" with a "Fine". They wanted to know more. I would guess they wanted to be close to their children, and they wanted to be able to help them if anything negative had happened. They wanted to be a resource and a confidante. They felt shut out by the cryptic answer.

Some people I have known feel that questions are intrusive, probing in uncomfortable ways. I imagine we have all experienced this feeling in the face of questions. Other times you are touched by questioning by how a person is taking the time to be truly interested in you or what you are interested in. I suppose that it goes without saying that moms want to be close to their children. Generally, their questions are of this variety. Sometimes, though, questions can be fear-based or imply an element of *checking up* on their teens that can ripple into the teens feeling judged and/or not trusted. Questions can also be accusatory, "Did you call to see if it was ready before you drove all the way down there?" "Didn't you see the sign?" These types of questions are not for information but most often to alleviate our own frustration over another's seemingly illogical behavior.

The use of appropriate questions and the understanding of the purpose of questions can aid in communication. I know this may sound like too much work or a bit contrived; but when we are trying to help teenagers cross the great divide into adulthood, extreme measures are sometimes needed!

The first step is to reflect just briefly on why you are asking a question. What is your motivation? What are you hoping for? Closeness, sharing, conversation, information based on fear of what your teenager may be hiding? When you know what you want, it is easier to ask the right question or maybe abandon questioning altogether and use a more direct route which I will talk about later.

If your motivation is conversation or just sharing with your child, you need to ask a more specific question. For example: "What are you doing in your English class?" "Which teacher do you like the best?" "Are any of your teachers boring?" "What did you do during your lunch break?" Just one, not all of them at once!

The second thing you can do is to share a short personal remembrance of high school. "I remember my history teacher in sophomore year—poor guy—we used to make fun of him because he repeated himself and couldn't always remember what he was talking about." Or a story in which you didn't look all that great yourself. "In high school I always felt so stupid in math because all of my friends were in the higher math classes and I wasn't."

If you are concerned about your child and fearful about what may be going on with them, it is better to take a more direct approach. Questions alone will probably not reveal the issues. When you are concerned that your child isn't doing well in school, they are having friend issues, or they are depressed or getting involved in drinking or drugs or *are over their head* in sexual activities, then it is often best just to say how you feel or what you have noticed.

For example: "I'm worried about you because you seem so much quieter than you usually are." "I'm concerned that you might be in over your head at (school, with your boyfriend, alcohol, fill in the blank)." "I know I can also worry about you just because I remember how hard my teenage years were and I love you so much." They may say, "No, I'm fine." They may yell, "Just leave me alone" and leave the room, but if you are truly worried, you will pursue the issue. You may say, "I know you don't want to talk to me right now, but I can't just ignore my feelings, so when can we talk?" In a serious case, you might say, "And if you don't want to talk to me, you have to talk with someone. Who will that be?" Then you offer alternatives acceptable to you: maybe an aunt or uncle they are close to that you trust, a therapist, a counselor or school psychologist at their school, a youth leader, or pastor at your church.

One caveat is that if you are always worried and constantly talking to them like this, then you probably need the help, maybe not them. Perhaps you need to get into a support group for parents of teens or talk with a friend who has a teenager or work on the stress in your own life.

But if your child is truly flailing, then our job is to throw a life preserver in after them. We don't rescue them, but we scaffold options for ways to survive and flourish.

My oldest son, of course, has taught me many lessons. Not intentionally but through parenting him, I have become a better person. When he was an older teen, he taught me probably the most valuable lesson. I wanted to be close to him, of course, but was not feeling that emotionally close. My idea of closeness includes sharing intimate details and feelings from your life and having the other person do the same. First, I need to mention he is by nature a quieter, more introverted person than I am, and next he is male. So right off the bat we have two different approaches to the world. My modus operandi would be to say something like, "How come you don't tell me things?" or "Why don't you tell me things?" I'm sure some people may be cringing as they read this. At some point I realized this felt like a criticism to him, that he wasn't doing something right. It also could feel like pressure to think up something to share.

Finally, I realized that if I asked him, "Do you feel close to me?" he would say, "Yes, just being together makes me feel close."

It occurred to me that if I perceived that closeness was sharing thoughts and feelings, I could do this. I could start, so to speak. I could do what made me feel close. I didn't have to make him feel bad; I could just do what made me feel good and close. So, I started sharing more intimate thoughts with him. I did what made me feel close, and oddly enough he started doing more of that too. He still felt close watching a movie together, but periodically he was open to *doing closeness* my way too. All of this was done without ever directly talking about these things with him. Instead of giving him the message, "You're not doing closeness the right way," i.e., my way, I just did it my way and left his response open. I could be me and he could be himself. It works much better this way. He taught me that people do closeness differently and it's OK to do it your own way. This knowledge has benefitted me in all my relationships.

I have heard it said, "You know you are mature when you can learn something from your child." Bingo, I'm there!

WHY? DOESN'T GET YOU THERE

In interacting with our children of any age, communication is the key. Communication is a skill, like any other. In order to build a skill, you need knowledge and practice. One element of understanding, the purpose of communication, is to find out what the other person's thoughts, feelings, and motivations are. When we are looking for understanding of our teenager, we often ask *why* a young person did a certain behavior.

The *why* question seems as if it should get us where we want to go—understanding—but in fact the question *why* often leads us to judgment and lack of understanding.

Just imagine yourself driving down the street; you make a left turn when you meant to go right. Your partner in the car might say, "Why did you turn left?" Are they really asking *why?* Often why means, "How could you be so stupid?" or "How could you do something so wrong?" If you don't believe me, just track for a week anytime someone uses the *why* question and see if you don't become a believer. When a child hits his brother, we say, "Why did you hit your brother?" The child's response is either a shrug or "I don't know." It didn't get us to the information we desired. A teenager doesn't do their homework and is failing a class. "Why haven't you been doing your homework?" Same response—a shrug. They aren't going to say, "I didn't feel like it." or "I felt like hitting my brother." The *why* question has only one response when it is asked in these situations, I believe. The answer is, "Because I'm a human being." In other words, that's why I make mistakes and do negative things sometimes, because I'm human. But that is not the answer we seek. We are looking for understanding of what was behind the behavior so that we can help the person find a solution.

The question that can get you where you want to go is, "What happened?" In all cases, you will receive more information with this question than *why* and yet *why* seems to be our default or go-to question.

Another helpful response to receive understanding may be *narrating*. In this case the parent just states what they saw or states the issue. "You haven't been doing your homework and you are failing your class."

Then you wait. You don't launch into a tirade or a teaching. You wait. Or "You slammed the door." Or "You're telling your brother a lot of negative things today."

The third method is *reflective listening*.

Either reflect back the feeling, of what they say, or express a feeling they might be having:

Your teenager gets in your car and says, "School sucks, I hate it." You reflect back: "School was a real drag today." (Don't say anything else; just wait.)

Or "You look like school was awful today," or "You look irritated." (That's all; then be quiet and wait.) If they complain and yell, just listen. Don't correct or try to teach or admonish now, even if they are saying outrageous things. Be quiet or just nod and make empathetic sounds.

These are techniques that do not come naturally to us. We need to practice. They will, in fact, get you to what is going on in your teenager much more effectively, though, than *why* questions or generic questions.

To recap:

1. When there is trouble to confront, ask, "What happened?"

2. Just narrate what happened or what you see.

3. When you want to help, use reflective listening.

A calm tone of voice and a serene atmosphere also can help, but this can be difficult when there is an issue to confront. Just remember, a negative emotional tone on our part is usually about us and will not lead to understanding of the other.

HOLD ON, OR LET GO— I WON'T GIVE UP ON YOU

Today I was speaking with someone who works in the probation department with adolescents in another state. He was explaining to me some of the processes that take place when a teenager (before 18) commits a crime. If it is a minor crime and the family has been assessed as relatively competent, the child may be held under house arrest in their home. The young person can go to school but must be at home or with the parent for the rest of the time given, as the consequence.

In a case he dealt with, a fourteen-year-old was put under house arrest for a minor crime. Unfortunately, he was involved in a crime involving a hold-up with a gun with his older cousin soon after his house arrest began. Now he is essentially in juvenile prison. His first thought was that the parents did not do their duty, or so it appears. Why was this fourteen-year-old out with his cousin?

I imagine these parents love their child. In his first experience of committing a crime, one has to wonder what his parents did to assess what need he was exhibiting through this behavior. What did they do to insure this young man got the lesson that his behavior would not be acceptable? Obviously, I don't know the full story, but the fact that they had not followed the monitoring procedures alone gives the message, *this isn't that important.* One crime—parents need to come down hard and serious. Two crimes—maybe the parents don't have the skills to find out the need and to set up consequences and communication to let their child know, "I won't give up on you."

Many years ago, when I was very young, before I had children, my husband and I had an opportunity to work for a court with convicted drunk drivers. I taught six-week courses to first offenders. My husband, a psychologist, was given a year-long therapy group of offenders who had more than one drunk-driving arrest. (The consequences are much more severe today.)

It was clear after a few months of doing this work that the people who had one arrest for drunk driving were so frightened by what they had done and so awakened by the experience that most of them were never going to do it again. They paid their consequences and learned their lesson. It was just as clear that the folks who had been arrested more than one time were alcoholics. In other words, they had a problem with alcohol which needed much more than just a scare.

If I could tell you all their stories, you wouldn't know whether to laugh or cry. Some people were quite creative in how they allowed themselves to drink and drive. One man had alcohol in the windshield wiper water container used to wash off his windshield, and he had rigged a tube to suck on that came into the car so that he could drink as he drove. He was one of the ones that did not yet think he had a problem with alcohol.

Most of them denied having problems with alcohol, and a few were trying to get help through AA. Adults have many choices. Society gives consequences, but we can't make a person change.

A fourteen-year-old needs us to help find out what motivates this behavior, what is the need. They need communication and consequences. They need by our monitoring and consequences to get the message, "I won't give up on you."

The young man in my story needed parents who decided to take *house arrest seriously*. They needed to set up a system where he was, in fact, monitored all the time, possibly involving other outside family members and friends. He needed to write about what he had done and the present and future results of his actions. Maybe he needed to make amends to someone or someplace, like cleaning graffiti or volunteering for the store that he tagged. He needed lots of listening and talking to see what he is missing that he thought he could fulfill through this behavior. Was it, attention, competence, significance, power, prestige, status? He needed stories of other people's mishaps and where it led. Maybe he needed a field trip to county jail. But he did not need parents who seemingly gave him the message by their lack of monitoring that his first crime was no big deal.

Teenagers are not adults; they are not mini-adults. They have the capacity to think in complicated ways, but they need to exercise that muscle and ability through the example and guidance of an adult, or several adults on the planet. The ability to think logically, hypothetically, and abstractly does not automatically mean you are good at it in the beginning. As a matter of fact, this new ability, actually, should give us pause. It is time to monitor and guide in different yet very specific ways.

The strategies here are the formulas for walking with our children through the teenage years, not taking completely over, not ignoring, but knowing when to lend just one finger, or a hand or a hug, when to follow their lead, when to grab on, and when to let go.

SCHOOL—I WON'T GIVE UP ON YOU

When my daughter was in high school, she took calculus. At one point she complained that it was difficult, and she couldn't do it. Let's just say I was not the one who could help her. What is a parent to do? Do I just tell her, "I can't help you?" I am her strategy teacher, remember. How does one tackle problems when they face them?

Her brother, who is a math whiz, unfortunately lived far away at this time, although I did suggest she call him on the phone. I asked her to talk to her math teacher and tell him of her troubles. Being a teacher myself, I know that when a student shows the initiative to ask for help, as an educator you have a good feeling about this student. After all, educators go into the business generally to help people! Human nature is human nature, and as a teacher if I know someone is trying, I am more likely to help them and to give them the extra point or so, if there is a dilemma.

Sure enough, she found out her teacher stayed after school two days a week for an hour to help students. Yes! Another strategy I told her was to find a student who was doing well and ask to study with them. Or I could find a student at the school who had already passed calculus and pay them a little money to tutor my child.

In other words, I don't do nothing, because "I won't give up on you." When I know things that you need to be successful, I will help you find them. Some of these strategies she took to college with her. Many times, my shy daughter went in and talked to professors about a class, an excellent strategy for success!

When our children go to school as kindergarteners, the teacher will generally give them homework. The idea educationally is to set a pattern that will serve them well later, that you need to study outside of actual school time. Another reason is to involve parents in the education of their children. With a five-year-old, the parent needs to sit down with the child and help them do their homework, not do it for them but sit close to keep them on track. Each year after, we begin to move ourselves away from sitting next to them to just being available for help and monitoring, slowly step-by-step giving them more responsibility for their own homework. Even in high school, students need parental monitoring on homework or school work. The school takes responsibility for letting us know our child's status through progress reports and grades, but/and we need to be interested and involved in their education.

Here are some more ways to help a teenager in this regard:

1. Pick something specific to ask about. For example, "What are you reading in English?" "What is the teacher having you do after you read?" "Are you learning anything in Biology that is interesting to you?"

2. Have your child explain something to you that you don't understand from looking at their book in any subject.

3. Read a book that the student is reading so you can talk to them about it.

4. Scaffold their experience. Once my daughter was crying about an essay she had to write, saying she didn't know how to start, etc. I asked to see the assignment, which was an essay question. Mind you, I hadn't read the book, but I just asked, "What do you know about this question? Just tell me anything you know about it." She started talking about it and I added what I thought they might be asking and asked her, "What else do you know?" And minutes later she said, "I know, I know, I'm fine. I know what to do." I didn't tell her what to write. I just scaffolded her thinking and jump-started her brain!

5. If they complain about or if you know they are having a test you can ask, "Would you like me to help you study by asking you questions or something?" Or, "Could I be any help to you in studying?"

BLANCA'S MOM

A few years ago, I had a student in my Child Development class who had a brilliant mother. Blanca's mom was a single mom. She was an immigrant who did not speak English well. In her country she had not had the opportunity to go to school beyond sixth grade. Blanca was raised in a very low-income situation, but she had a loving and bright mother.

Blanca was a very capable and intelligent young woman. She did well in class. Her family situation did not fit into the profile for success in school. What was the secret that set Blanca apart from many of her cohorts?

When Blanca was a child and into her teenage years, Blanca's mother supported her education in the best possible way. While many others in her situation told their children that they couldn't help them in school or with their homework because they didn't speak English, Blanca's mother used brilliance.

When Blanca was to do homework and when she came home from school her mother would say, "You're so lucky that you have the chance to learn. Tell me about what you are learning." Blanca's mother loved learning. The fire behind her words told Blanca that learning is the exciting element. Her enthusiasm wasn't focused on school or getting ahead, or I can't help you. Her brilliance was the brilliance of showing an enthusiasm for knowing things, for learning things, for wondering about how the world works. Two messages Blanca received loud and clear: *Lucky you* and *learning is an enjoyable part of life.*

Blanca would have to explain to her mother what she read or what she was working on or what she had learned. The benefit to Blanca was real learning. There is an old saying, "Teach what you need to learn." So as Blanca taught her mother what she had learned, she was essentially studying what she needed to learn. In the explanation to her mom, she was solidifying her own knowledge and gaining understanding as she heard her own words and had to put into words all that she was absorbing.

The love of learning is an enrichment to life. The force of this we are born with. You can't stop a young baby and child from learning without tying them up! We come into the world primed to learn all about the planet we have been put on. During the course of schooling, unfortunately, sometimes this love is derailed by feelings of inadequacy in the face of learning things that prove difficult for us or are difficult in the time allotted. We are required to learn things we may not be ready for or that we are not particularly interested in, at least not right now. Sometimes this leads to children equating learning with school; and if they don't like school, they may believe falsely that learning is not valuable. We make a mistake in our language, I believe, when we say we need to make learning *fun* for children. Learning is fundamental to our very humanity, and all we need to do is model that enthusiasm in our own lives, a *let's find out, I wonder* approach to life. Blanca's mother had that in spades. Your child explaining what they are learning in any language is learning.

Blanca also felt a sense of her own power and pride as a learner—confidence. "I can teach my mom things, Wow!" Seeing yourself as a capable learner we know is half the battle in school success (and life). So, through her ability to be the leader, the *teacher* with her mom, Blanca became an adept learner. She increased her own understanding of facts and ideas. She honed her communication skills and developed vocabulary. She became an expert life-long learner. Blanca did well in school because she had a brilliant mother who knew what gift to offer her daughter—the enthusiasm for life and understanding the world, an enthusiasm for education, a respect for education as the institution which tries to open-up this world in varied views.

Another consequence of their exchange was quality time with her child. Through the sharing of knowledge and ideas, Blanca and her mother spent time together that was focused and close. They weren't just watching a TV program sitting side-by-side but were engaged and intent, and together.

The love of learning was the gift that kept on giving. It provided quality time for them. Blanca and her mother were learning, Blanca did well in school, and she gained confidence in her abilities. The repercussions snowballed. Blanca's mother deserved the *parent of the year award!*

RUNNING AWAY OR TO?
I WON'T GIVE UP ON YOU

I once read a story about a little boy being asked to write about his weekend and running off and hiding under a desk. The teacher unfortunately punished him for not finishing his work. Later an assistant, who had more insight to this very clear physical message the child had given (hiding), was able to talk with him as he shared that his weekend included the police coming to his house and taking his Daddy away. Behavior is motivated by need. When I hide or run away, I am giving a message. Can you read it? It's not always crystal clear what message is being given, but be assured it is a strong message.

The removal of the whole body from a situation is a fairly dramatic act. I'm not accepted here. I'm not respected here. I have no response that is powerful enough to be heard, so I will run and hide.

Teenagers often feel powerless in relationship to their parents. We have been the *gods* of their life. They thought for many years that we knew everything and could handle everything well. In our changing relationship to them as parents, we also may feel powerless. They may tell us less or make choices we wouldn't have made, but we need to remember we have a very deep and strong emotional power over our children, no matter the age.

The difference at this age, though, is that they act as if what we say doesn't matter to them very much. To be your own person, whom they must become, you want to try to feel as if you are wise enough to make your own decisions. Even though we may feel they are not, it is time to support their feeling that they are. That is, if you still want to have any influence at all, you need to respond to this developmental stage with messages of trust, hope, and love.

When the teenager removes their body or runs away, this is a red flag, of course. What is the message?

We have all run away at one time or another, I'm sure, stormed out of a house or a car, gone off to get away. What were you feeling then? A guess would be that it was precipitated by an interaction where you came out on the bottom. In your own mind you can't face something or someone. We fight when we don't feel safe. We will often flailingly do whatever we can to feel safe again, even if it means being alone. When a teenager runs away, there is something they can't face at home or within themselves. Running away is very internal, personal, and implies the element of hiding something they can't share or deal with. In a way, running away is a means to keep the person intact. If it is an internal issue, they will learn the old-adage, *wherever you go there you are.* But as a teenager they are more vulnerable to these internal concerns and, therefore, we want to be more observant of their behavior. They often don't have the experience, perspective, or words for these first-time strong feelings. We can help them filter, act as an anchor, and be an example of a seasoned adult.

When we receive a strong message, it requires a strong response. Our strength is in listening, being responsive. What does this child need at this time?

Our response needs to be honest and confrontational. In other words, don't ignore the behavior or just yell or just put restrictions on the young person (remember the little boy under the table).

You might say, "I was so worried and scared that I didn't know where you were. You really needed to get away." Then listen. If they don't talk you need to say, "That was a pretty strong statement. I know you wouldn't worry me for no reason, so I know there is a very important reason that you ran away." Listen. Make a statement of what happened or what you think they may be feeling and then wait and listen.

By affirming that they had a good reason, or they wouldn't have done it, you show them respect. You validate that their choices, in fact, have meaning whether or not we understand the meaning. Through this approach they are more likely to share the motivation or the need. The benefit for the young person is self-understanding and connection. Through connection you have a better chance to influence what actions they take next.

It could indicate that you have not given them enough power in their life. You have too many restrictions. It could be that they don't want to do some of the things you believe are necessary; and they feel if they tell you, you will be angry or withdraw your love. It could be they don't feel accepted for their choices and their ideas. Of course, it could be it has to do with something going on in friendships and school, but I would guess the act of running away from home has more to do with what is going on in the home than in the outside world. The inability to share what is going on in their world because of your reaction would be another reason, but this still indicates the inability to face you and whatever else is happening.

When a red flag is waved, to ignore it could land you gored from behind by the bull! The flag is a message and must be read as such. By confronting the flag, we teach our child that danger signals can be confronted; we have choices. A red flag is just a warning, not a death sentence. Warnings heeded empower us to take ahold of this one life we have control over, our own.

Remember this message is, "I won't give up on you."

CONTROL — FINDING YOURSELF ON THE WRONG ROAD

Sometimes I have heard the mothers of young teens getting involved in gangs being quoted as saying, "There is nothing I can do." I want to say, "Maybe not now," even though I don't really mean this, because there is always something you can do. What I mean is that communication, relationship-building, and respect for the child as an individual really should start in the very beginning of their life. It is something constructed over time so that, in fact, you have a huge impact on how your child behaves based on your relationship.

One of my pet peeves in the education of educators is the use of the words, *controlling* the children's behavior or *controlling* a classroom. I understand its use is to mean behavior-management techniques. I do believe a teacher is the manager in the classroom, but we are not in the business of controlling people. In my view, our language is very important in this regard, as it creates the framework for our thinking which reflects in our actions. Our goal is to have people grow up to reach their full potential and add to society and not take away.

The feeling of wanting to control another's behavior, of course, is understandable. I'm sure you've been in the position to see clearly what someone *could* do to save themselves some pain in life. You give this tidbit to the other as advice... and they ignore it! They don't do what you suggest. In other words, I hope by now you know you can't control others. As a matter of fact, if we put out the feeling of trying to control, we usually get a reactionary stance from the other person, no matter the age. Especially this is true of people in the business of defining who they are, i.e., teenagers.

As parents, when we are desperate, we sometimes try to control or use strong-arm tactics; but in situations you can't control, don't make rules you can't follow through with or monitor. Don't give up your power or act in a way that shows personal weakness, but don't come off like a dictator, just a strong person.

For example: what if your teenager says, "F--- you." Can you actually make him stop? No, but you can say this, "I don't allow people to talk to me like that, and especially people who I love. I feel so hurt that you would talk to me like that." Say it and turn and walk away.

When your child comes back later to apologize, which I think they will, you can say, "I still feel hurt so if I act a little strange, that is why." If they don't apologize but just try to act like it didn't happen, I might say, "You know I feel hurt by what you said." Wait and see what they say. Don't act as if nothing happened; it did. Your child showed a great disrespect for you and hurt you. When people hurt people, there are consequences. The most powerful consequence is in the heart of the *hurter*—the negative feeling they have about their own behavior. The relationship you have with each other will lead to reconciliation through honest communication of feelings. You don't need to yell and scream and act as they are acting; this will breed more negative outcomes and less teaching.

When our children were in high school, the idea of an open campus for lunch became a policy of the school. Parents had to sign a paper if they *did not* want their children to go off campus for lunch. I remember my husband saying that signing that paper was useless because this behavior was not something we could really monitor. It would be better to have the conversation about your real feelings about off-campus lunch, your concerns, etc.

For example, "I'm not going to sign the paper restricting you from off-campus lunch, but what do you think some of my worries might be about it?" Ask them. Add to what they might say. "I know sometimes kids get pressured to ditch school after lunch if they go off campus or they go to someone's house whose parents aren't home. I worry that you *might* be pressured to do something you don't want to do. I also worry about traffic and cars when a bunch of teenagers are driving around, etc. and are distracted by their friends. I guess I'm worried about your safety and any pressure you might feel, too."

So truly the conversation and the relationship are the powerful elements. The respectful, honest exchange of concerns is a similar dialogue you might have with a best friend as an adult. Teenagers are ready for this because of their new ability to think abstractly and hypothetically. Once again, you are also modeling how to handle feelings.

A huge responsibility of the adults on the planet is to model what to do with our emotions. By the time you are two, you have definitely had every human emotion possible, but you are uncivilized and haven't had much experience with what behavior can follow these emotions. Emotions are not *bad* but clearly behavior can be negative. I would venture to say that most people who are in jail for actually committing crimes have not learned appropriate behavior to deal with their emotions. Many people in doctor's offices might be able to say the same thing: think ulcers, colitis, and asthma; even cancer and heart disease can be exacerbated by stress and emotion that has no positive outlet. A murderer's anger is no bigger than yours; it's mainly an issue of how to channel it.

It's never too late to go back and redo. You can't rewind or erase like in the old days, but you can press the *refresh* button. Tell your child, "I've been thinking about, a) how I handled what you said or b) what I've said and now I want to say something else or something different," for example. It's never too late to be genuine with your blossoming adult.

I won't give up on you or myself either. All of us are in the *formative* stage called life.

VI

Lessons
Learned

THE WORST PARENTING STORY I'VE EVER HEARD

On a Friday afternoon a friend of mine showed up at my home and said her 14-year-old daughter had gotten into a fight at school and the school wasn't doing anything, so she was going to call the sheriff in town. Of course I was shocked and asked for details. The school principal had told the girls that she would meet with them first thing Monday morning, so to me it seemed the school was *doing something*. What ensued was the worst parenting story I have ever heard.

The two girls had no guns or knives or threats. It was a typical, *why are you flirting with my boyfriend* type of verbal altercation that ended in some pushing and hitting. I questioned the wisdom of going to the sheriff and shared that the school would probably deal with it on Monday. I actually felt the sheriffs would probably be laughing behind her back if she showed up with such a story.

She, in fact, ignored my advice and went to the sheriff, and I believe they listened politely but told her there was nothing they could do at that point.

The reason I believe this is the worst parenting story I have ever heard is because at this beginning stage of womanhood, she is essentially saying to her daughter, "You can't handle this situation and I, your model of womanhood, your mother, can't handle this situation either. We will have to call in the big guns, generally the men perhaps."

One thing you don't want your teenager to believe at the beginning of their adult life is that they can't handle it. I believe she was undermining her daughter and herself. Her job as a parent is to empower her daughter to handle life, not to tell her at the early stages that she can't! In this story, there is the potential for creating a victim! You do not want your child going into the teenage years believing they are a victim. Here was a perfect opportunity to listen to her daughters' story, to ask her daughter what she thought she should do with this girl, what strategies she could use to face this person. Believe me when I say that this will not be the last time she faces a difficult person or a downright idiot. A parent needs to help their children develop ways to deal with all of life's challenges.

Whenever our child complains about another child at school at any age, our first support is to listen without judgment or advice. Use our reflective listening and don't intervene with *lessons*, at this point. I know it is difficult to remember, but this is their life, not yours. Some parents confront the other child themselves, some call the child's parents in anger, and others tell their child what to do. None of these strategies will help them in their life, and handling it yourself often leads to an embarrassing situation of adults acting like children. Your job is to help your child know how to handle their own life in effective ways. This is a gift you can give your child. Believe me, this is much more adaptive and ultimately satisfying than yelling at another child or parent!

Our next move is to ask them what they think they should do about this situation. How do you think you can handle the girl? What do you think you could do in this type of situation in the future? What are your choices? What did you learn? This should only take place after we have fully listened to their feelings, which might sound irrational at first. We call that venting, and it can be perfectly healthy and appropriate with a loving, accepting listener, which is your role.

Additionally, at this point if you have given the former strategies the time they need, you can have input of other ideas your young person might use. If they have left out a strategy that you think would be useful, you can say, "Something you might try…" or "I've seen other people try this…" Stay away from, "You should do this." A lesson is much more useful if we invest in it. Resist the urge to be the great *fixer*, which is a strategy that handicaps our child. If your child comes up with an idea you think will be disastrous, talk them through the outcomes or consequences. For example, "If you do that, what do you think will happen then?" Continue this line until they have thought of all the outcomes. Also, you can ask them what they think would be the conclusion they would like to see from this experience.

When my oldest son was in sixth grade, he complained about a boy down the street bullying him and teasing him on his way home from school. He was a year older than my son. I knew the boy a little but not his parents. One day I got upset and marched angrily toward their home, knocked on the door, and said that their son was bullying my son. He was there and I told him, "Don't ever do that to my son again," in an angry voice.

I always regretted my behavior. I saw the boy for years and each time felt embarrassed and really ashamed that I didn't handle it differently. I was just venting my feelings like a mother lion, and I did not use the opportunity for lessons for either child or for good relationships in my neighborhood!

Another strategy that I could have applied in this instance, if the strategies of my child handling it on his own did not work, would have been to calmly go to their home with my son and ask if we could all sit down and talk, parents and young people. I could have modeled good communication by having my child say how he felt to the boy and his family, and by asking what they thought we could do about it. It would have been an effective conflict-resolution model and a strategy they could have used other times in their lives. We would have probably all felt fine afterward and not embarrassed to be around each other. I failed as an adult on the planet that day to rise above my animal instincts and teach my child how to be a person.

CAR ACCIDENT — LEARNED MY LESSON

When my son was sixteen and on his first date with Nicole, we got a call at 11:00 p.m., and my son's teary voice said, "Mom, I could have killed her! I was in an accident." I felt a certain calmness because they were OK and I knew that my son had learned a lesson that night, a lesson I had tried to teach with my words since he had begun to drive. I can kill someone in a car. Lesson learned. He now understood the lesson, so what was my role as a parent? My main concern as a parent is to help the growth of a person throughout childhood to become a productive member of society. There are so many lessons to learn and he had, this night, learned a very valuable one.

As we met the father of the girl for the first time at the scene, I was nervous about his reaction; but he was a kind and gallant individual who said, "I crashed a car when I was a teenager." His empathetic reaction was another lesson for my son.

My son, as consequences, had to go to the hospital all night while she got stitches in her arm, bring her flowers the next day, and apologize to her parents. He had to pay the insurance deductible and take care of the towing of the car and interfacing with the insurance company, but there was no punishment, much to the chagrin of his older brother. He had learned his lesson in the first minutes after the accident. It's my job to teach him lessons, not to beat his mistakes over his head or make him suffer. If he had said, "Oh, it's not that big of a deal; no one really got hurt," I would have had different consequences to make sure that the lesson was learned. At least this one time, it was parenting at its best.

The consequences of his actions were adult consequences, taking responsibility for the accident. When a teenager, or any child learns a lesson and you know they have or they can articulate it, your consequence is done.

If he had just called and hadn't shown that he understood, we could have asked him to tell us what he had learned from his experience, or to write what he had learned; and then we would know if the lesson, in fact, had been learned. If the lesson hadn't been learned, he probably would have been restricted from driving. We could say, "It seems you don't understand the seriousness of the potential of car accidents. It seems to me then that you aren't ready to take on this huge responsibility, so you won't be driving for a month, but I'm sure you will learn through your reflection on all the consequences."

There is nothing to be gained and much to lose by punishing a young person who already understands. To me this is the height of disrespect. Possibly you have been the recipient of this type of *beating* as a child or even as an employee or spouse. The idea is you just keep reminding the person of what they have done and try to punish them over and over with it even though they already feel badly; they already know what went wrong. In other words, they get it! The reminder of our mistakes or wrong doing by others only causes resentment and, in fact, takes our attention away from the lesson that we need to learn and focus on. Sometimes what people remember about this type of haranguing is the words or yelling but not, in fact, the lesson that they personally learned.

An adult friend vividly remembers having a third-grade teacher hitting his held-out palms with a ruler. I asked him, "What did you do wrong?"

"I have no memory of that," he said.

Opportunity missed. You desire them to bow to the lesson in gratitude, not resentment, as they put this *knowing* in their pocket for another day.

ELECTRONICS —
YOUR QUESTIONS COUNT

In a parenting class for parents of teens, a woman mentioned that their internet had gone out, all their bundled services—gone. While her twin fourteen-year-olds complained bitterly, the family ended up spending time around the table discussing the history of the civil rights movement in the US, a subject her children were studying in school. Mom lamented that it was the best night they had had as a family in a long time.

I admit I am looking at my phone as I wait for my Starbuck's or any time I have a momentary lull in my life. I tease my college students by saying, "I don't know how anyone gets a date anymore; it used to be during the break, the cute guy next to you would talk to you." Anytime we have any break in class you will see forty faces immediately go to their phone. Electronics are a convenience, a joy, and a bane to our lives. The issues surrounding media are plentiful. The locks that can be put on phones, internet and TV, I would recommend until your child is fourteen or so, or longer if you desire, but there is no reason to be too uptight about the reality of our lives. The pull is there; as in all aspects of our children's lives, it is how we handle it that really matters.

Sue Bender in her book, *Everyday Sacred*, asks the questions: "Why be unhappy about what you have control over and why be unhappy about what you don't have control over?"

Too much emphasis on restriction is not helpful, too much protection is not helpful, and too much nostalgia about how *things used to be* is not helpful.

It is the information age; we all have a computer phone connected to us at every second. It is incredibly useful to find a fact, find a product, find a movie, or find your way, but all things have multiple sides.

We have choices, of course, but it is a seductive instrument. Using locks, etc. on certain programs that come into your home is a fine idea, but it goes beyond that to once again have the conversations with your child. Along with the elements of disconnecting from each other by staring at a screen constantly (enough has been said on this in other places), there are other forces to consider and reflect on with your child. They remember what we say if it is done humbly, and they remember when we listened.

Reflect with your child about what is the life they want. What is quality of life? What do they think that would look like? How would their vision affect others around them? John O'Donoghue said, "Live the life you love." What does that mean? Look for quality in your input; look for images, words, thoughts that help you to live the vision you have for your life and leave the rest. So humbly ask the questions that we all should consider. The ability to have an examined life sets us apart from other animals. Maybe there is a reason we have this ability?

I will never forget the picture I saw of a starving toddler, laying listlessly with extended stomach. I will never forget the pictures of burned humans after the Hiroshima bomb was dropped. I will never forget the pictures of stacked bones in a group grave from the Holocaust. Maybe this is a positive, since these pictures help me to be sensitized to horrible, destructive elements of our present and past world. Maybe they motivate me to act in ways that prevent future pain. But are there pictures I can carry around in my head that may be destructive, of sexual brutality or exploitation and degradation? Do these images harm one's sensibilities as too much violence on media can desensitize us to its horror? Even computer programmers will tell you, *garbage in, garbage out.* What do you want in your beautiful mind, child of mine?

If you have been on a trip that has been planned to the finest detail from pictures you have seen perhaps or places you have heard about, yet, you might note, when you get home, your stories of your trip often will be about the delightful surprises, the unexpected encounters, and the serendipity. Information can only go so far in a quest for a beautiful life. Knowledge of a sunset, or a rainbow, or sexuality itself does not make it valuable. Information is necessary and empowering and fruitful, but it is not everything. Information tempered with room for discovery is a much more satisfying human experience.

Once an older friend of mine shared that her husband had been diagnosed with a heart problem that he would probably die of, but there was nothing they could do about it. I remember thinking, is that a good thing to know? Do you just sleep with your hand on his chest for the rest of your life? Many people would say it is better to know what you are facing, but sometimes I wonder if there are limits.

Once a doctor told me to get an abortion because of some health risks that I had. He gave me all the information and I thanked him. I also asked that he not bring it up again during my pregnancy because I was going to go ahead with the pregnancy. He was respectful of this. In my case, later research showed that he probably overreacted in his advice. OK, he gave it his best shot at the time, but sometimes I wonder.

Even in an emergency room recently with a friend, the doctor said that the CAT scan he had showed every little thing but not to worry about some of the small indicators. Once you know, it is difficult to then *not* know. Is there such a thing as too much information? I believe in my life there has been some evidence this may be true.

In other words, wonder with your child. Examine your feelings and thoughts aloud with your teenagers—not your answers but your questions. Some I may have raised above. As you watch with them, talk about the concerns that you truly have about what you see or have heard about certain media.

The popular show *Married with Children* was on in the late 80's and most of the 90's. I told my children they could not watch it. I never wanted them to think that the way that couple talked to each other had anything to do with what marriage should be. I didn't want that type of disrespect as part of their image of relationships. Many people I have told laugh at that; even my children now laugh about it, but they also know exactly what about the show I found offensive, especially for young people forming their ideas. So I did the right thing. They got it. Did they ever watch the show? I know they did when I wasn't around, but they never forgot the values I put into their heads along with it. Pick your values and communicate them in a humble way. Your concerns are the fodder from which their own morals and ideas will grow. It is very powerful stuff that many parents forget about. Your power is in your relationship with your child. The power lies in the *how*.

Monitor and negotiate time and content when possible. Let them know what shows and internet content you find objectionable and why. The *why* is the important element. So tell them they can't watch certain shows and why you find them objectionable. Will they ever watch them when you are not around? Probably, but now they have the content of your values in their head as they watch. It is a huge difference in their ability to see and make judgements. Can you explain your values about life to them? *You* are the reference point, or would you rather leave that to the TV or internet.

Our input matters, even if they appear not to listen, our feelings and thoughts are very meaningful and powerful to our children at any age.

I HOPE YOU LUCK

I hope I have changed your mind about teenagers; I hope I have reminded you of the titanic forces within your child. I hope I have touched your heart with empathy and given you a renewed and knowledgeable direction for your relationship with your child.

Through your words and actions, you can let them know that they matter, they are significant, a person, *you like.* They are *cherished* for who they are *now.* Spending time with them is valuable to you. When they pull away you continue to be the interested parent you have always been.

Through your words and actions, you communicate that their *choices have meaning,* as they are looking at options to figure out their theories about the world. The choices they make are not frivolous, even if you don't agree with them. You have faith in them to navigate it well.

Through your words and actions, you show them, *you won't give up on them, ever.* They need to know that what they are feeling is just right on, normal, no matter how scary and uncomfortable it feels. They see reflected in you, a hope for who they already are.

I believe these messages are vital to your teenager. I hope you feel the same; you are empowered now to be the bearer of the support they need to grow up emotionally healthy. I believe in you!

Recently I told my granddaughter of something I had to do that was a little difficult, in her four-year-old empathetic voice she said, "I hope you luck." I pass it on to you!

ABOUT THE AUTHOR

Nancy Washburn, M.A., is a Professor and Vice-Chair of Child and Family Studies at LA City College.

For the past twenty years, Ms. Washburn has taught Child Development classes to thousands of young adults across the greater Los Angeles area. Her goal as a professor has been to inspire new teachers and parents to use their knowledge to help children and families to be the best together, and for society. Prior to teaching college Ms. Washburn was a Parent Educator for sixteen years with families of children from birth through adolescence. Ms. Washburn has taught a variety of workshops on Parenting, Conflict Resolution and Guidance. One of her favorite jobs has been raising three children of her own into productive human beings.

Throughout her career she has been spurred on by her own confusion and lack of confidence as an adolescent and the desire to help young people and their parents have a smoother ride. In writing this book she enlightens parents and gives them the knowledge and messages they need to have a positive relationship with their child. The messages promote healthy attachment and facilitate young people in being secure within themselves and in the world.